The Modern Blacksmith

The Modern Blacksmith

ALEXANDER G. WEYGERS

Illustrated by the author

VNR VAN NOSTRAND REINHOLD COMPANY
New York   Cincinnati   Toronto   London   Melbourne

On the front cover

TOP PICTURE:
- 1 bowl-carving gouge
- 2, 3, 4, 5 large-size woodcarving gouges
- 6 decorative wall hooks
- 10 forged blank for a large shallow wood gouge
- 11 hand-forged needle-nose pliers
- 12 extra-wide flat woodworker's chisel
- 13 wide-jawed plumber's wrench
- 7, 8, 9, 14 medium-size woodcarving gouges
- 15 samples showing oxidation color spectrum on steel
- 16 garden tool
- 17 kitchen spatula
- 26, 25, 18 mild-steel hammers to be used with stonecarving tools
- 19 one-point stonecarver's tool
- 20, 21 stonecarver's claws
- 22 stonecarver's bush tool
- 23 center punch
- 24 cold chisel
- 27 group of small engraver-style woodcarving gouges
- 28, 29 rawhide hammers to be used with medium-size woodcarving gouges

BOTTOM PICTURE:
- 1 one-piece fireplace tong
- 2, 10 fireplace pokers
- 3, 8, 9 various sizes of fireplace shovels
- 6 stove-lid lifter
- 7 short-handled adze
- 11, 12, 4, 5 hammers converted from standard hammer heads to shape specific curves into specially made forming swages

Van Nostrand Reinhold Company Regional Offices:
New York Cincinnati Chicago Millbrae Dallas

Van Nostrand Reinhold Company International Offices:
London   Toronto   Melbourne

Copyright © 1974 by Litton Educational Publishing, Inc.
Library of Congress Catalog Card Number 73-14101

ISBN 0-442-29362-3 (cloth)
ISBN 0-442-29363-1 (paper)

All rights reserved. No part of this work covered by the copyright
hereon may be reproduced or used in any form or by any means — graphic,
electronic, or mechanical, including photocopying, recording, taping,
or information storage and retrieval systems — without written permission
of the publisher. Manufactured in the United States of America.

Illustrations by Alexander G. Weygers

Published by Van Nostrand Reinhold Company
A Division of Litton Educational Publishing, Inc.
450 West 33rd Street, New York, N.Y. 10001

16 15 14 13 12 11 10 9 8 7 6 5 4 3 2

Library of Congress Cataloging in Publication Data

Weygers, Alexander G.
  The modern blacksmith.

  1. Blacksmithing. I. Title.
TT220.W48   682'.4   73-14101
ISBN 0-442-29362-3
ISBN 0-442-29363-1 (pbk.)

Contents

INTRODUCTION 7

TWO MAKESHIFT FORGES 8

1. The Blacksmith Shop and its Equipment 10

The Forge 10
The Blacksmith's Fire 11
The Water Dipper 12
The Anvil 12
The Blacksmith's Vise 13
Hammers 14
Tongs 14
Steel for the Blacksmith 15
Blacksmiths' Coal 16
Containers for Quenching Liquids 16
Auxiliary Tools 16
Recommended Power Tools 17
    THE MECHANICAL STEEL-CUTTING SAW 17 / THE ABRASIVE CUTOFF MACHINE 17 / CUTOFF DISCS 17 / THE LARGE MOTOR GRINDER 18 / THE COTTON BUFFER AND THE ROTARY STEEL BRUSH 19 / THE DOUBLE-ENDED ARBOR 19 / USING THE DRILL PRESS AS A WOOD LATHE 19

2. Hammer and Body Motions in Forging 20

Practicing Correct Hammering 20
Use of Forging Hammers 21
Use of the Sledgehammer 24

3. First Blacksmithing Exercises 26

Straightening a Round Bar 26
Squaring a Round Bar 27
Tapering the End of a Squared Rod 28
Shaping the End of a Square Rod into a Round-Cross Section 28

4. Upsetting Steel 29

Upsetting a Rod End To Form a Bolt Head 29
Use of the Upsetting Block To Form a Bar Tool 30
Forging a Hexagon Bolt Head 31
Correcting Upsetting Errors 32

5. Upsetting with the Aid of an Upsetting Matrix 33

Making an Upsetting Matrix 33
Upsetting Steel into Bolt Heads with an Upsetting Matrix 34
Making a Carriage Bolt Heading Plate and Decorative Bolt Heads 35

6. How To Temper and Harden High-Carbon Steel 36

First Method of Tempering 36
    THE FILE-TIP TEST FOR HARDNESS AND TEMPERABILITY 36
Second Method of Tempering 37
Third Method of Tempering 38
Drawing Temper Color 38
Quenching Liquids 38
    EFFECT OF QUENCHING LIQUIDS ON HOT STEEL 38

7. Making a Right-Angle Bend 40

Making a Jig To Forge a Right-Angle Bend 42
A Right-Angle Bend Using Vise and Jig 43
Making a Right-Angle Bend in a Mild-Steel Angle Iron 44
Making a Right-Angle Bend in a High-Carbon-Steel Angle Iron 44

8. **Some Tools that are Simple to Forge and Temper 45**

   A Cold Chisel 45
   The Cape Chisel 45
   A Crowbar 46
   A Center Punch 46
   A One-Point Stonecarving Tool 46

9. **Decorative Treatment: Rosettes and Wallhooks 47**

   Decorative Rosettes 47
      PATINATION 48 / OTHER SIMPLE
      DECORATIVE FORGINGS MADE FROM
      SCRAP STEEL 48
   Freehand Curving of Steel 50
   A Decorative Wall Hook 51

10. **Hinges 52**

    Making a Hinge Without Machining 52
    Ornamental Hinge Designs 53
    A Gate Hinge 54
    A Hinge Made from a Leafspring 54
    Hinge for a Woodbox Bench 54

11. **Hold-Down Tools 55**

    How To Use the Hold-down Tool 55
    How to Make an Adjustable
    Hold-down Tool 56

12. **A Fireplace Poker 57**

13. **Fire Place Tongs 58**

14. **A Spatula Made From a Section of Coil Spring 59**

15. **A Door Latch 61**

    First Method: A Slotted Jig 61
    Second Method:
    A Spring-action Die Set 61
    Third Method: A Vise and Bar 62
    Making the Button on the
    Door-Latch Bolt 63

16. **Making an Offset Bend in a Bar 64**

17. **Blacksmiths' Tongs 65**

18. **Making Milling Cutters, Augers, and Drills 67**

    A Milling Cutter 67
    Augers 69
    Wood Drills 69
    Drills for Cutting Steel 69

19. **Stonecarving Tools 70**

    One-Point Stonecarving Tool 70
    Two-Point, Three-Point,
    and the Claws 70
    Bush Tools 70
    Drifts 71
    Cleaving Chisel 71

20. **Wrenches 72**

    Open Wrenches 72
    Box Wrenches 73

21. **Accessory Forging Tools 74**

22. **Woodcarving Gouges 75**

    A Cone-shaped Gouge 75
       SHAPING THE BLADE WITH
       STANDARD SWAGE 76
    Correcting Common Errors in the
    Forging of Gouges 77
    Veining Gouge 78
       MAKING A DIE ASSEMBLY FOR THE
       VEINING GOUGE 78 / FORGING
       THE GOUGE BLADE 79

23. **Forging a Pair of Pliers 80**

24. **Making a Fireplace Shovel 82**

    Basic Principles of Forming
    Heavy-Gauge Sheet Metal 82
    Forming a Shovel Blade 83
    A Decorative Steel Shovel Handle 84
    A Large Fireplace Shovel 84

25. **Making a Small Anvil from a Railroad Rail 86**

26. **The Power Hammer 89**

    PHOTOGRAPHS 90
    GLOSSARY 94

Introduction

The art of blacksmithing, beginning before recorded history, has changed very little over the centuries. In the recent past it reached such a peak of perfection that it will be difficult to attain that excellence again. But the very fact that our present society has entered into a renaissance of handcrafts now places the skill of working at the forge in a most promising light.

Modern equipment and trends have introduced new elements into this age-old art of hammering iron into various shapes on an anvil. For instance, that very useful new device, the visegrip pliers, is a very welcome additional tool in the modern blacksmith shop, not replacing traditional tongs, but supplementing them.

The utilization of salvaged steel material is a modern phenomenon. The present "economy of waste" has created an abundance of discarded, high-quality steel from scrapped automobiles and a variety of mechanical and industrial equipment. This gives the contemporary blacksmith excellent material at almost no cost. In addition, modern power-tool equipment (secondhand or new) can be repaired or converted to meet specific tasks. Soon, an ideally equipped workshop comes about. No matter how "junky" it may seem in the eyes of others, it enables the modern blacksmith to forge useful and beautiful things from a seemingly endless variety of salvaged scrap.

Some years ago I set up a good, but simple, blacksmith shop in my second-story sculpture studio in Berkeley, California. All I had was a 100-pound borrowed anvil mounted on a wood stump; a coal fire in an ordinary wood-burning stove; a standard household hammer; a pair of visegrip pliers; and a 1/4 hp motor, salvaged from a discarded washing machine, with which I drove my grinding and buffing wheel unit. Limited though it was, I had sufficient equipment to make my own sculpture tools for wood- and stonecarving.

The modern blacksmith must learn to do by himself that which the old-time blacksmith and his helper did as a team. So it is this I am proposing to teach here: how to resort to whatever we may invent, improvise, and construct in order to reduce the handicap of not having an apprentice helper.

In all of these activities, the machine plus modern hand tools become our assistants. Hand-filing, hand-drilling, and sledging can easily be replaced with the power grinder, table power drill, and power hammer. Nevertheless, the forgings do not necessarily need to assume a mechanized look. If the machine remains strictly the helper, the overall results remain hand-rendered in appearance. The modern blacksmith who truly loves his craft will scrupulously want to perfect his skills in pure forging. Machine "hypnosis" must always be held at bay so that the craftsman will remain in full control of the machine and not the other way around.

Although I was taught the several methods of welding, I have purposely eliminated this aspect of metal work because, as I see it, blacksmithing, without welding of any sort, is the "mother art" in forging. I believe that, like good wine, the pure flavor of the craft should remain undiluted.

Forge-welding, once mastered, becomes too readily the easy way out, like a short cut. It is used primarily when joining two or more separate elements together, and in the recent past was overdone by tacking on this or that endlessly. For those who want to learn forge-welding, there are ample sources to encourage and teach this craft. (Unfortunately for the forge-welding purist, the field has had recently to contend with the acetylene torch and electric arc, which have made it obsolete.)

The mechanical welding field is a thing apart, and I leave it to others.

Decorative wrought-iron work is simply an offshoot of blacksmithing. So is horseshoeing. Doing either one does not make a blacksmith. Ornamental work and sheet-metal practices are only touched upon in this book in order to round out the general activities in the shop and to acquaint the reader with their possibilities.

The illustrations in this book are meant to represent, as nearly as possible, live demonstrations in the shop. They are intended to show *how* something can be done: not the *only* way, but one of many possible ways. They therefore are not to be considered as inflexible blueprints; instead, the craftsman is encouraged to *improvise*, using these basic guidelines for his constantly expanding skill as he works at the forge. Above and beyond showing *how* something can be done, *why* we do what we do is stressed as of overriding importance.

The student of pure blacksmithing will find this to be a no-nonsense book. Practicing the progressive steps will result in an independent craftsman, able to make "things" out of "nothing" in his simple shop. The promise of success, then, is limited only by the talent and enterprise of the beginner, and not necessarily by the lack of expensive or elaborate equipment and materials.

TWO MAKESHIFT FORGES

Many years ago, in Lawang, Java, I had an opportunity to try out some rare wood for carving. The forestry department there had given me a freshly cut section of podocarpus wood (about 24 inches long by 20 inches in diameter) which I had selected from their samples for its very fine grain and ivory color. But I was warned that the wood was subject to severe checking during drying, and I hoped to meet the problem by first roughing out the composition and then hollowing out the core, leaving a uniform thickness so that the remaining layers would check insignificantly.

My problem, however, was how to make the tools for the carving and hollowing out. I was able to purchase, for a few pennies, some old, worn files as metal for my tools at the native marketplace in the nearby village of Porong. And, luckily, I located there a blacksmith shop where the smith allowed me to spend the day forging the tool blanks. The shop was primitive, but, after all, forging is mainly confined to the simple requirements of fire, hammer, and anvil.

Charcoal was the fuel for the fire. There were a few worn hammers. The anvil had no horn, but there were a few round, heavy, broken steel

Village blacksmith shop in Java, Indonesia, 1935

little boy pumps 2 cock's feather & reed pistons in bambu tubes

fuel: teakwood charcoal
anvil: broken shaft of sugar mill crusher, set in wood stump
forge: basin & air ducts in clay
quenching tub: hollowed out log
shop: bambu structure & clay floor

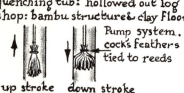

Pump system. cock's feathers tied to reeds

up stroke   down stroke

—15"—

the tool was forged & tempered in the above shop

rods to be used instead. And so, in the same amount of time it would have taken me in a modern shop, I had soon finished my tool blanks.

The illustration shows how the native blacksmith shop actually looked. Not shown is the feeling of kinship the Javanese smith, his little boy, and I had while working side by side as we shared the common language of this basic craft. The final result was the needed large tools and the carving of the lifesize wood sculpture shown on page 90.

Ten years later I again had to improvise a way to make some needed tools: a set of small woodcarving gouges and some engravers' burins.

I had settled in a small cabin in the woods in California where, as yet, I had no workshop and no electricity. I was limited to a few implements: a small machinist's vise; a pair of pliers as tongs; a table-clamped hand-grinder; a heavy bulldozer part on a stump as my anvil; a regular two-pound carpenter's hammer; and a bucket of water for quenching. Charcoal from the doused embers of the fireplace was my "blacksmith's" fuel.

I made my forge from a coffee can with an opening cut in the side and air holes punched in the bottom. This I attached to the lower end of a 12-foot-long, 5-inch-diameter steel irrigation pipe, given to me by a farmer friend. I hung it from a tree branch, and the draft up the pipe fanned the charcoal fire in the can, giving me my forging heat.

With this setup I forged the little tools which made it possible for me to do the sculpture carving and the engraving on wood shown in the photographs on page 90.

outdoor arrangement to forge small artifacts

salvaged farmer's irrigation pipe used as chimney

can is filled with charcoal. & removable pin holds can to chimney

fire

water bucket

salvaged part of a bulldozer used as anvil

charcoal made from fire place hot coals snuffed out in airtight can

small tools easily forged in above setup

1. The Blacksmith Shop and its Equipment

semi-dark blacksmith shop

practical home-made forge

THE FORGE

Blacksmith forges, with hand-cranked air blowers, are still being made and can be ordered new through some hardware stores. If you are lucky, you may find a very useful old one secondhand. However, a simple forge is not difficult to make from available salvaged material. The examples shown here are only a few of a great variety. You may very well invent your own setup, just as long as it accomplishes its basic function.

The basin holds in its center a sufficient mound of glowing coal in which to heat the steel. The flow of centrifugally fanned air entering from below can be controlled for a fire of less, or more, heat.

A hand-cranked centrifugal fan is good. One driven by an electric motor, controlled by a foot-pedal rheostat switch, functions well. Even an old hair-dryer fan, without the heating element, can be adapted to do the job.

It is here that the question comes up: which is preferred, a hand-cranked blower or a machine-driven one? My preference has always been for the hand-cranked blower. It has the self-governing feature of the air flow stopping automatically when you stop cranking.

If you use an electric fan, make certain to install a foot-operated rheostat which shuts itself off once the foot is removed. Such a switch automatically stops the air flow, and the fire remains dormant while the smith is forging.

If you use machine-driven blowers without a foot-operated rheostat, use a damper in the air feed. It should have a spring action that automatically shuts off the air flow when the foot is removed from the damper pedal. A mechanically driven system without such a safety device requires remembering to shut off the air flow manually each time forging is to begin. To forget invites a dangerous situation: an ever-growing fire at your back while you forge. In your absence it may radiate so much heat that it could ignite nearby paper or cloth, or burn steel left unattended in the fire. *Make certain your forge is of a type to prevent overheating of a temporarily unattended fire.*

The modern improvement of a hinging smoke-catcher is an additional desirable feature for a forge. It is similar to the antipollutant device in some automobiles. In cars it catches oil smoke and leads it into the combustion chambers of the engine. In the forge, the smoke emission, mixed with surrounding oxygen when starting up the fire, is led by the catcher back into the fire by way of the air intake. Once the fire flames up, it consumes the smoke by itself and the smoke-catcher, no longer needed, is hinged out of the way. A relatively smokeless fire is maintained thereafter.

In my student days in Holland, we had the old-fashioned, overhead leather bellows. The lower chamber pumped air into the top chamber, which stored it under pressure. This still remains a good system, as are all types of blowers that accumulate air in storage bags or chambers, to be released under even pressure. If you plan to make or restore one, note that such bellows should not be less than four by five feet.

In arranging the shop, keep the forge, anvil, water trough and dipper, tong and hammer racks, etc. so spaced that simply by taking a single step you can pick up what you need while working between the forge and the anvil. No time is lost then, and forging can begin within one or two seconds after the hot steel has been pulled out of the fire.

The forge and tools should be located in the darkest part of the shop, so that the heat of the steel can be judged correctly, in a semi-dark space. In broad daylight too hot a steel can hardly be seen, and overheating may then ruin it structurally. This is why the outdoor rivet-heating forges, used in bridge building, always have a shading hood to shield the fire from sunlight. These little forges, if you can find them, are ideal in a hobby shop. They are completely adequate for the size of most forgings described in this book. Only when large pieces are to be forged will a more sturdy and roomy forge be needed. Then the whole setup will require a more specialized type of shop, with a more elaborate array of accessory tools.

THE BLACKSMITH'S FIRE

Keeping a medium-sized fire clean and effective all day long is one of the more difficult skills for the novice to acquire. Strange to say, what seems at first the least of our problems in the blacksmith's craft — starting and maintaining the fire — often proves to be a stumbling block for the beginner. But in due time it becomes routine, and experience will cancel out the initial frustration.

In the day-to-day work of blacksmithing, each previous coal fire leaves a remnant of coke, small cinders, and ashes. Smoke and yellow flame indicate the burning of unwanted elements that are not pure carbon.

Coke is what coal becomes after it is heated. Like charcoal, coke lights easily and gives off a blue flame. It makes a "clean" fire. A "dirty" fire (one which still smokes) should not be used in heating steel, since it harms the composition of the steel.

Slag is a melted mix of noncombustible matter in coal. It lumps together at the air grate below the fire, often plugging up the holes and obstructing the flow of air, thus lowering the fire's required heat. Each time, before starting a fresh fire, remove the slag from the air-grate holes with the point of the poker.

Ashes and small cinders will drop through the air grate into the ash pit below the forge. This built-in ash pit should have an easy-release door

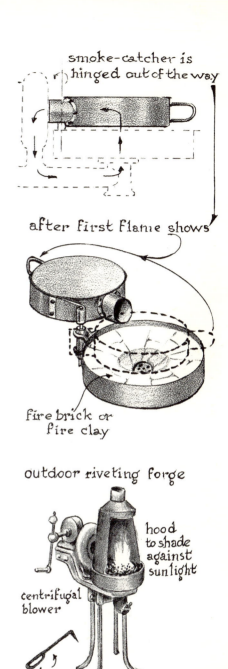

smoke-catcher is hinged out of the way

after first flame shows

fire brick or fire clay

outdoor riveting forge

hood to shade against sunlight

centrifugal blower

poker

fresh coal

coke

air grate

ash release

so that its contents can be emptied into a metal bucket below, or fall in a heap on the dirt or stone floor. (In these accumulated ashes I often poke a piece of hot steel that needs to be very slowly annealed.)

To start the fire, use a handful of wood chips, or some coke left from a previous fire. Fill the surrounding spaces with ample fresh coal. (If it is in large lumps, break it up into pea-sized pieces.) This surrounding coal is the supply which will be raked into the going fire from time to time to replenish whatever has been consumed. It should be kept wet with the sprinkler can so that the fire will not spread out larger than is needed. Blacksmith coal is expensive, so be economical with it!

Crumple half a sheet of newspaper into a fairly tight ball. Light it, and place the burning wad on the cleared firegrate, holding it flame downward with the poker. *Gently* crank the air fan with the free hand until the flame is burning well, then crank vigorously. Now let go of the fan and, with the freed hand, rake the ready coke or wood chips (but not the fresh coal) over the flaming wad of paper. The fan meanwhile idles by its own momentum; when cranking is resumed, the paper wad is fanned into still more vigorous flame.

At this stage the greater amount of smoke can now be caught by the smoke-catcher hinged in position over the fire. Some smoke is bound to escape, but will soon change into flame. When the flame breaks through, hinge the smoke-catcher hood out of the way.

Now let the fire become evenly hot before raking in some of the surrounding fresh coal. It is best to rake in only a little of the fresh coal from time to time to avoid smoke emission; a yellow flame that combusts the smoke is preferable to having to use the smoke-catcher too often.

Throughout the many years that I have forged tools and artifacts, I have rarely needed a *big* fire. In old blacksmith shops, however, I have experienced entirely different situations, where the blacksmith had to weld and repair heavy equipment. His forge had a fire twice as large as we need. Therefore, if you should find, inherit, or purchase a large, old blacksmith layout, the first thing you should do is reduce the space around the air grate by about one-half. The economical way is to start with a small fire, enlarging it only when specially required.

Gas-fired forges have several disadvantages: noise, excessive steel oxidation and a large fire-grate opening through which small workpieces become easily lost. I always avoid them in favor of the simple coal and coke fired forges.

THE WATER DIPPER

A water dipper can be made from a one-pound coffee can nailed onto a wooden handle (a small tree branch will do). The bottom is punctured, with a fine-pointed ice pick or 1/32-inch nail, with holes about 1/2 inch apart. The dipper is used like a sieve for sprinkling water *slowly*. As a water quencher it can wet down coal, or the part of the steel that sticks out of the fire, to keep it from overheating, especially when steel is held by hand instead of with tongs.

THE ANVIL

Some hardware stores will still take special orders for anvils, but prices run high.

During patriotic frenzy in past wars, anvils that had been neglected in farmyards and old shops were given to the government to be melted into weapons, making it almost impossible to find one secondhand today. (Already, however, the blacksmith had practically been replaced by mechanized industry.) The limited number of available used anvils are often quite worn, or severely damaged, and have to be refaced. Consequently, you may have to make do with any hunk of scrap steel (35 pounds or more) that is suitable to forge on. The illustrations show the shapes of makeshift anvils that I have used quite satisfactorily. It is also possible to make an anvil from a section of large-gauge railroad rail (how to do this is shown in Chapter 25). Therefore, the lack of a professional anvil is no reason to postpone your first experiences in blacksmithing.

Secure the anvil, or a substitute, with bolts or spikes, on a block of wood or tree stump. The height of the block plus the anvil should be such that the knuckles of your fist, with arm hanging freely, just touch the face of the anvil. At this height a hammer blow can strike the steel at the end of a full-length arm stroke.

Always keep in mind that whatever is used to "pound" on can never be too heavy. An anvil must never be so light that a hammer blow can move it.

anvil made from scrap railroad rail

correct height of anvil on stump

THE BLACKSMITH'S VISE

The gradual abandonment of equipment from old blacksmith shops has left fewer and fewer used post vises available. New ones can still be ordered, of course, but at great expense.

A heavy *machinist's bench vise* (35 pounds or over) will do very well for a simple shop. If you should be lucky and find a secondhand 100-pound monster (even a somewhat damaged but still functioning one), do not hesitate to acquire it. The heavy mass of a vise (as with the anvil) must be great enough that each blow on the hot steel held in it will be fully effective.

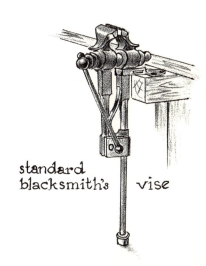

standard blacksmith's vise

standard machinist's bench vise

HAMMERS

Blacksmiths' hammers are available through hardware stores and mail-order houses. They have changed little in design, although the steel composition may have improved through modern metallurgy.

The cross-peen-type hammer is the most useful. One end of the hammer has the cross peen, which is used to draw out steel, while the other end has a flat, octagonal face, slightly rounded off at its edges to leave an almost circular face. The face itself is very slightly convex, so that any minor inaccurate blows by the hammer's edge, not parallel to the anvil face, will not leave deep local markings in the steel.

Several hammer sizes (weights) and designs are used, but the beginner will not need more than a few at the outset.

The *flat and cross peen,* and the *flat and ball peen* are the all-round blacksmiths' hammers. Sizes of 1, 2, 3, and 4 pounds are preferred. Any specially shaped hammers you will learn to make later on (see chapter 21).

The heavier hammers, as a rule, are the *sledgehammers.* In olden times the smith had his apprentice helper to swing the sledge when heavy stock was to be forged. There is a limit, therefore, to the weight of hammer you can use by yourself. If you can acquire a small-caliber mechanical hammer, it will do the heavy sledging for you (see chapter 26).

TONGS

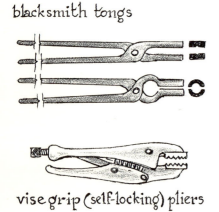

You can see old collections of tongs displayed in blacksmiths' shops in museum towns such as Williamsburg, Virginia, and Sutter's Fort in Sacramento, California. They are of every conceivable size and shape, revealing how the smith would make a special pair for each new forging problem. The jaws are made in infinite variety, to hold each particular steel workpiece firmly and easily during forging. And today, as in the past, there is no limit to the usefulness of having many designs at hand as you work. You will learn to make a pair of tongs in the same way that the early blacksmith did, and thus gradually be able to build up your own set exactly as you want it.

The old smith did not have our modern visegrip self-locking pliers, a very welcome, practical addition to the blacksmith's shop. It can be used most successfully in place of the old type of tongs which had a clamping ring that held the jaws firmly together. Visegrip pliers can hold the widest range of sizes and shapes of stock during forging, more easily and better than the old tongs. I recommend them highly.

STEEL FOR THE BLACKSMITH

This book stresses the fact that excellent steel can be found in the vast scrap piles across the country. The salvageable items in their varied sizes, shapes, and qualities seem endless; waste is one of the U.S. economy's natural by-products. Gathering such waste can become a great pleasure, because finding anything one has good use for, that others throw away, is like finding treasure.

High-carbon steels are the choice items. In cars, all springs are of sufficiently high-carbon content (over 0.2%) to make such steel temperable: this means of a hardness to cut wood and mild steel. In all the years that I have made tools of such steel, I have never had one that disappointed me.

A most important source of steel is the auto-wrecking yard where scrap car parts are to be found; the useful ones include leaf springs, coil springs, starter springs, axles, valve springs, push rods, valves, stick shifts, steering cross-arms, linkage rods, torsion bars, and bumpers, and any and all items you *suspect* may be of useful size and shape (see photograph, pages 92 and 93).

The local auto wrecker is generally selling salvaged replacement parts from cars. He earns a greater margin of profit per pound of steel than the dealer in scrap steel. If, therefore, economy is your aim, go to the dealer who sells scrap steel *only*. If he allows you to roam through his yard, you can gather an incredible variety of items.

Bars and rods in all sizes lend themselves to making many forged items. Coil springs can easily be straightened under heat (as described on page 59). Sometimes flat steel, even if it has been curved, also offers the promise of good stock. Heavy-gauge old saw blades, (straight and circular saws and heavy industrial hacksaws), tractor plow discs, chain-saw bars, old files — all are excellent material for your collection.

Old rusted tools, such as cold chisels, carpenters' chisels, center punches, crowbars, and cleavers are useful, as are remnants of reinforcement steel and waste plugs that come from rivet holes punched out of plates at boiler factories and steel-construction plants. Abandoned farm machinery will prove rich in high-carbon steel.

Look also along highways and country roads. Big companies, as well as individuals, often seem to prefer leaving steel waste strewn around rather than carrying it off to the salvage yards. In this way, somewhat bent steel braces, bolts, bars, and plate from electric poles, overgrown with weeds, have found their way to my steel scrap pile.

Additional useful items to salvage are discarded ball bearings (barrels full are thrown out by electric-motor repair shops, garages, etc.). These lend themselves to making tools and jigs and makeshift instruments and a great variety of forgings. Old cast-iron pulleys, gears, and heavy items make good forming blocks on which to pound hot steel into curves.

Use your imagination in selecting items which might be useful for something or other. But be cautioned: store them inconspicuously. To your neighbor, your pile of scrap steel may be an eyesore. Keep it out of sight; and you will find that everyone will enjoy the finished treasures you make out of the things that once were just junk.

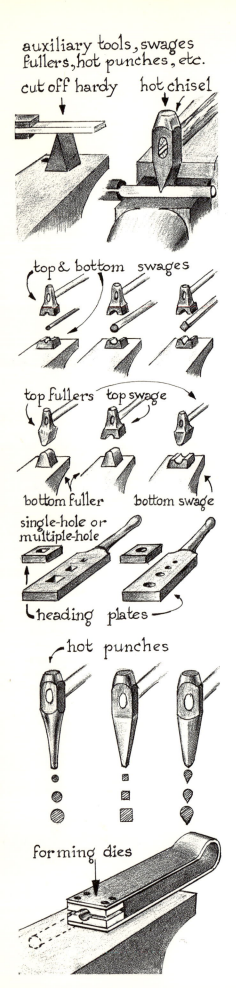

BLACKSMITHS' COAL

The coal we use is always called "blacksmiths' coal" to distinguish it from household coal. It is more expensive, but with correct use it lasts longer. It also burns hotter. It leaves clinkers (slag) instead of ashes and is therefore cleaner, releasing less ash dust into the air. Whatever its composition in scientific terms, the farmer's feed-and-fuel stores throughout rural areas that sell this coal always call it "blacksmiths' coal." As a rule it is sold in 100-pound sacks. It is this coal that is used by horseshoers (farriers).

CONTAINERS FOR QUENCHING LIQUIDS

The Water Trough or Bucket. This is for the quenching of hot steel to cool it or temper it. It should hold not less than five gallons of water, and should be deep enough so that a long, hot section of steel bar can easily be quenched.

The Oil Container. This too should be generously large, holding not less than five gallons. It must have a hinging lid that can be closed quickly to snuff out any flash fire. (Sometimes, through misjudgment, too large a piece of hot steel is quenched in too small a quantity of oil, which could bring the oil smoke up to its flash point.)

The oil-quenching container should remain either out-of-doors or in a separate area of the shop, away from wood or other combustible objects. A metal, or metal with asbestos, sheet should surround the forge and oil bucket, between them and the wall. If the floor is wood, metal sheet should cover it where hot steel or coal might fall accidentally. An earth or stone floor and walls are ideal for this area of the shop.

AUXILIARY TOOLS

Cutoff hardies, hot chisels, top and bottom swages of various sizes, top and bottom fullers, heading plates, hot punches, and forming dies all are useful and often necessary tools. These and others will be introduced in succeeding chapters as they are needed to make the things we want. The blacksmith's craft thus proves perfect for making just about any "tool to make a tool."

RECOMMENDED POWER TOOLS

The Mechanical Steel-cutting Saw

Although steel-cutting bandsaws and reciprocating hacksaws can be bought fairly cheap new, the hobbyist may be challenged to make his own.

I recommend converting a salvaged 12-inch-diameter woodworking bandsaw by first reducing the saw speed, following the scheme in the illustration. Bandsaw blades with fine teeth serve best. The hardness of the teeth is the same for the cutting of wood or mild steel; hardened steel must never be cut on such saws. (For hardened steel, use the abrasive cutoff wheel.) You will find that these worn, discarded mechanical saws, found in secondhand shops, generally have all their vital parts in good condition: the motor, wheels, bearings, pulleys, and adjusting mechanisms. The parts requiring renewal usually are the rubber wheel-linings on which the steel bands ride, the drive or pulley belts, and the two small brass guides between which the bandsaw rides.

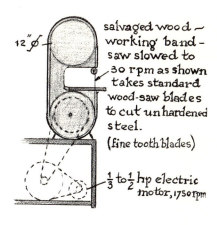

The Rubber Wheel-Linings. Rummage through a tire-repair shop's scrap can and salvage a large rubber inner tube. With scissors, cut it into large rubber bands the width of the bandsaw wheel. You may need two or three for each wheel. Forcibly stretch these over the wheel rim. If tight-fitting, they do not need to be bonded together with any cement, and the wheels do not need to be dismounted for this operation.

Drive Belts. Belts that are not too worn and frayed are often found strewn around auto-wrecking yards. Keep a collection in various sizes and adapt them to your shop improvisations for driving odd transmission setups.

Adjustable Brass Band-Guides. Remove the old ones (but only if you see that hardly anything is left to warrant prolonging their use). If no brass is available to you, salvage some harder variety pot-metal parts of cast instruments and machine housings found lying around scrap yards. They can easily be hand-sawed into the size of these insets. If you find that they wear down too fast, look for scrap fine-grain cast iron from which to saw out the parts.

The Abrasive Cutoff Machine

Follow the illustration exactly to make this indispensable tool for cutting steel of great hardness. The skeleton frames of many discarded home utility machines (dishwashers, washing machines, bench-level refrigerators) can be adapted for this purpose. In combination with the converted bandsaw, the two machines will meet all of your power-cutting needs, saving a great deal of time, as well as your back and energy.

Cutoff Discs

These can be located as waste items in large steel construction plants that use discs 18 to 24 inches in diameter, 1/8- to 3/16-inch thick. The washers that clamp these large, high-speed discs securely are approximately 6 to 8 inches in diameter. In time the part of the disc *outside* the washer becomes worn down to the washer rim, therefore becoming useless in those plants. Barrels full of the remaining 6- to 8-inch discs therefore become waste. The company will either give you some, or sell them to you for much less than if you had to buy them new in that size. These industrial wheels, being of the highest quality, will not shatter easily. Use 1750 rpm wheel speed as further precaution against accidents, however.

Although high-speed machines may save time, they are also more *dangerous*. After all, we are not in that much of a hurry. Therefore, a one-to-one drive by a secondhand 1750 rpm, 1/4 hp motor will work fine and be *safer*.

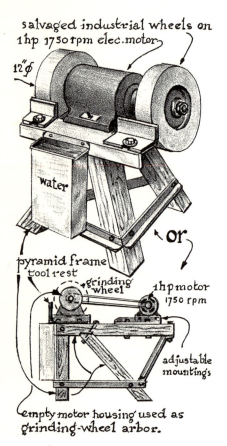

The Large Motor Grinder

Seriously consider having one large power grinder in your shop; it will give you great satisfaction. You might choose either one of the illustrated setups, whichever fits your personal circumstances.

First Example. Your electrical wiring must be able to pull a 1 hp, 110 V, 1750 rpm motor easily. Use secondhand remnants of industrial grinding wheels, about 2 to 3 inches thick, 8 to 12 inches in diameter. The setup shown has proved to be a very great asset around my shop. Once you have it, you will wonder how you could ever have done without.

Second Example. I have also used this system very satisfactorily, although it is somewhat more complicated to set up. The center part of the old motor housing is cut in half horizontally on the abrasive cutoff machine after discarding the motor's "innards." Both bearing sideframes are kept intact. Cut an opening in the rear center, for passage of the two belts from the driver motor to the pulleys mounted on the arbor shaft within the old motor housing. Reassembled, this is the finest sturdy arbor that one could wish for.

On the metal-turning lathe, turn a shaft to fit the salvaged motor bearings. (If you have no such lathe, you may need to get help on this.) Thread both ends of the shaft to receive a fine-grain wheel on one and a very coarse-grain on the other. Two V-belt pulleys are mounted on the center of the shaft.

The Cotton Buffer and the Rotary Steel Brush

You will find that these are invaluable mechanical devices. The arrangement shown is constructed from scrap pipe, with a ball bearing used at the ends. The buffer or steel brush is mounted on one end, and the other holds the driven pulley.

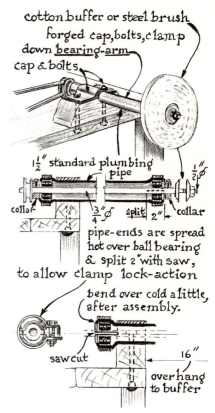

The Double-ended Arbor

A drill chuck is mounted on one end and the other may hold whatever grinding wheel is needed. (The table drill press can be adapted for this purpose, but it is preferable to have the double-ended arbor to save the drill press from overwork.) The arbor will accommodate the endless variety of small auxiliary insert grinding points, sanding discs, and sleeves. With it, the widest range of grinding problems can be met. Tool blades or odd-shaped freeform articles that start as blanks from the forge are rough-ground, then refined, on the double-ended arbor inserts, and finally polished on the buffer.

Arbors can be bought ready made through mail-order houses. Be warned, though, to avoid the types with plastic bearing sleeves that wear down in short order when abrasive grit dust gets into them. As a rule, sleeve bearings lack a good seal against abrasive matter. Make sure to choose only arbors with well-sealed ball bearings, if you can afford them. If a bronze sleeve bearing comes your way, improvise a simple seal with oiled felt wrapping, binding it around the bearings with string. This will be effective even if it looks junky. Always be sure to keep oiling holes closed against abrasive dust.

Using the Drill Press as a Wood Lathe

Temporarily converting the drill press into a wood lathe is a simple arrangement, particularly useful for those craftsmen keenly interested in expanding their projects with the making of carving tools. As shown in the illustration, the parts needed are not very difficult to make.*

With this setup, tool handles can be made without a horizontal lathe. However, well-functioning wooden handles also can be freely shaped with saws, chisels, and disc sanders, and often look more attractive than lathe-turned ones.

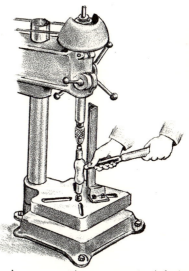

*In my book "The Making of Tools," Van Nostrand Reinhold, 1973, greater detail is given on this subject.

2. Hammer and Body Motions in Forging

principles in use of hammer & body motions, & body stance

hammer is above head at start

⊙ shoulder joint

Right

shoulder is down & stationary all muscles & joints are at maximum use.

You must try to make each hammer blow as effective as possible with a minimum expenditure of body energy. The way to accomplish this is not as obvious to the beginner as it may seem, but must be learned through practice, until it becomes automatic. Any effort that concentrates action in the shoulder alone should be avoided, as the illustration clearly shows.

You stand at the anvil with legs spread enough to brace yourself firmly, one foot a little back and the other forward under the anvil overhang. Bend your head directly over the anvil, but hold it a little to the side to make certain that the hammer swings safely past it. There is a real danger that the hammer, bouncing back from an accidentally missed stroke, could hit your head. At the same time, keep your head *close* to the work, in order to have a clear view of every mark made on the hot steel by the hammer. This allows you to judge where to strike next.

Caution: During such close work it is wise to *squint* your eyes to protect them from ricocheting steel particles or oxide scales. General practice and experience will prove that, thus protected, the eyes are seldom injured. However, floating cinders and ash dust, or little oxidation scales flying off the steel during forging, sometimes do get into one's eyes. The logical question is: should you wear *goggles?* My answer is to do so if you feel apprehensive, but realize that most smiths probably do not wear goggles during forging and would rather put up with squinting and occasional eye-washings. Without goggles we have a full 180-degree view of the shop. I myself only use them while motor-grinding steel. But take warning! You must use your own judgment, and hold only yourself responsible if accidents occur which might have been avoided.

PRACTICING CORRECT HAMMERING

Use a piece of cold mild steel as a practice piece. Hold it in your hand, or tongs, or visegrip pliers, and strike it with the hammer as if it were hot. Go through the phases of the hammering movements again and again to loosen up any awkwardness.

Take special notice of the exact finger and hand positions, as these "loosely" hold the hammer at the very start of the stroke. Its weight should first be held cradled in the crotch between thumb and forefinger, while the other fingers, standing a little outward, line up along the hammer stem. The hammer is angled backward. The first motion is the contraction of the fingers, giving the hammer its initial movement, followed by the arching path of the arm until the hammer meets the steel.

With an accelerating force, all the other muscles of the body now follow that first finger-pull. (The finger-pull on the hammer stem at the

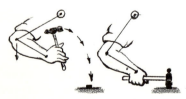

correct movements when using light weight hammer create a high-velocity "snappy" blow

start of the hammer stroke is also the required technique when riveting small rivets, or hammering delicate objects such as lightweight nails into fairly hard wood.)

The drawings aim to help the student visualize a live demonstration. The *wrong way* of hammering is also shown.

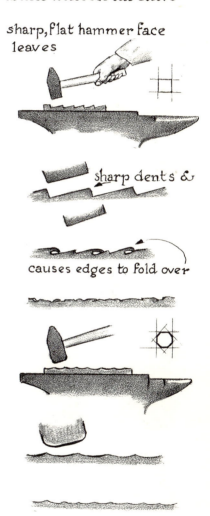

USE OF FORGING HAMMERS

No matter how skilled the smith, hand-hammering is always less accurate than machine-hammering. Therefore, the design of the hammer will affect the results.

A sharp-edged, perfectly flat hammer face will damage the surface of hot steel, making sharp dents and ridges. With continued hammering, the standing edges will begin to curl over in leaflike portions which, in turn, are pressed down into the steel below. The damage is multiplied progressively, resulting finally in a completely chewed-up surface. The only way to repair it then is by completely grinding off or filing away the damaged surface.

If the hammer face is slightly convex (crowned), with its edges somewhat rounded and its corners beveled to an approximate octagon, then the hammered surface is indented without sharp edges. It leaves only shallow concave impressions (valleys) and gentle, low ridges (summits). Continued hammer blows with this same hammer will *compress* the summits into succeeding shallow valleys. A skilled smith, working to refine that nearly flat surface, will apply gentler and gentler precise blows until finally an almost accurately smooth flat plane results.

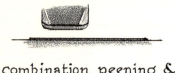

combination peening &

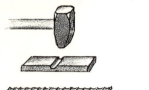

flattening

draws out steel fastest

On thin steel the flat — but not sharp-edged — hammer face can safely draw out (stretch) steel. On *thick* steel, the cross peen is more effective. It draws out an even surface with firmly pronounced ridges, but not as sharp as the ridges left by using a sharp-edged flat hammer face. Off and on, the hammer, in uninterrupted movement, is flipped into reverse position in mid-air so that the next series of blows are struck with the flat face on the ridges left by the cross peen, until gradually the steel surface becomes approximately flat once more. This alternating treatment is repeated as long as enough heat is left in the steel.

peening one side only curves a bar

Since drawing out steel means stretching it, hammer-peening on one edge of a flat bar inevitably curves the bar, with the resulting thinner edge outward. Further stretching that side, by flattening the ridged surface with the hammer face, will curve the bar still more.

drawing out steel
(stretching thick into thin steel)

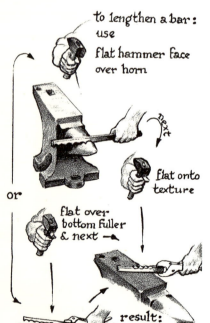

to lengthen a bar: use flat hammer face over horn

Next

flat onto texture

or

flat over bottom fuller & next →

result: before after

There are several methods of drawing out steel from thick to thin, narrow to wide, and various combinations, such as widening a piece in all directions while making it thinner.

To lengthen a bar without use of hammer peen, place the heated bar over the anvil horn, and pound with the flat face of the hammer. Next place the steel on the anvil face as shown, and hammer the ridges out flat. Continue drawing out the steel in this way until the desired length is reached.

Another way of drawing out is to place the bottom fuller in the hardy hole and hammer the bar out on it instead of on the horn. Flatten ridges on the anvil face, etc.

To widen a bar, use the peen end of the hammer spreading the steel *sideways* only. While there is still enough heat, flip hammer over in mid-air, as described before, using the flat face to drive down the ridges left by the peen. This stretches the workpiece sideways once more within one heat.

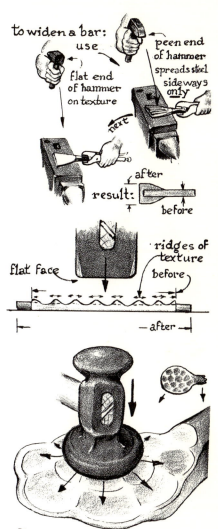

To spread the steel in all directions, first use the ball end of the ball-peen hammer, then the flat end, to spread the steel outward from the center.

It is now logical to add to the variety of hammers in your shop to allow yourself a wider choice: sharp- and obtuse-angled peens; small- and wide-diameter ball peens; shallow or more convex face, etc. Still greater variety can be obtained by adding hammers in different *weights*. The double ball-peen hammer, with two different peen sizes, is one of the most useful ones for making the blanks for woodcarving gouges (as described in Chapter 22).

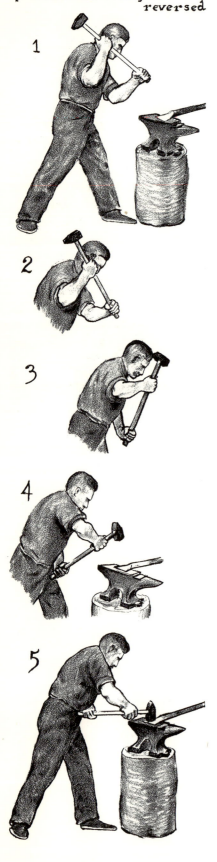

correct use of the sledge hammer
position of feet may be reversed

1
2
3
4
5

USE OF THE SLEDGEHAMMER

The use of a heavy (4 pounds or over) sledgehammer simply speeds up the work of forging large volumes of steel. In all hammering, body motions should combine a maximum precision of aim with the stored energy in the hammer blow.

The stroke begins with the right hand fairly close to the left hand, then sliding toward the hammer head as the stroke progresses. The drawings (steps 1 through 5) show the progression of the hammer's path and body motions during one cycle. This lets the hammer head enter into a *spiral curve* instead of a more or less circular arc. It is done by a very skilled sledger if he feels certain that by thus increasing the energy storage (the hammer head moves into a larger outer-diameter curve and therefore a longer path) he will not sacrifice the accuracy of the hammer stroke. It is this sort of combination of body movements that create a whiplash effect to increase energy storage.

Various combinations are possible, depending on the skill of the sledger. He can lift the hammer with right hand held close to the hammer head and then, letting the hammer head slide outward, bring both hands together at the end of the hammer stem. Or he can hold this final position for the maximum path of the hammer. The only danger is that the sledger might miss in his aim in this large swing.

A yet greater sledgehammer swing (not shown, since rarely needed) was practiced in olden times when the blacksmith had helpers. This was the overhead, full 360-degree swing. In my training years I often used skilled fellow student helpers, sometimes three of them simultaneously, each meshing his own cycle into the uninterrupted overhead sledging of the others during the period of one heat. It was an exhilarating experience as well as a practical way of drawing out or upsetting heavy-gauge steel parts. Circus gangs use the overhead swing with large diameter wooden (often steel-weighted) malls when driving tent stakes into the ground. You can practice heavy sledging similarly, by driving a heavy stake into the ground. Once this is well learned, practice also the 360-degree overhead swing on such a stake; you might at some time have to use this skill in helping a smith at the anvil.

The logical next step is to use the cross peen of the sledge to draw out steel. But try this only after you have learned controlled use of the sledge's flat face. *Caution:* If you should miss, and the corner of the cross peen strikes the anvil face or its edge, it may be dented or broken, a very serious setback. Such misuse can cause irreparable damage to the anvil, your work, or to *you*. You will not regret having a 6- to 8-pound sledge in the shop, but do not underestimate the necessity of knowing how to use it safely. Naturally only *heavy anvils* can take the powerful blows of heavy sledgehammers.

correct use of the sledge hammer's cross-peen when drawing out a wide bit at end of a heavy bar

7½ lb

← 4 lb
← 7½ lb
← 16 lb

heavier sledges to be used on heavier anvils

3. First Blacksmithing Exercises

How does the smith judge quickly each next move when he must "forge while the iron is hot"?

The student blacksmith will learn that when steel has reached forging heat, success depends on three things: *precise judgment, perfected skill,* and an instinctive *feeling* for what is right or wrong. Combined, these enable him to act decisively at the right time. When the moment has come to apply his knowledge and skill, he cannot afford to hesitate, doubt, or let the time to act pass by. He must do *then and there* what needs to be done.

A blacksmith works with hot steel that is as malleable as clay. Steel, made soft, can be pushed together (called upsetting) to make a piece *shorter and thicker.* Or it can be stretched out (called drawing out) to make a piece *thinner and longer or wider.* Therefore, both a blacksmith and a clay modeler think in somewhat similar terms when it comes to judging how to change a given volume of material from one shape into another shape. The only difference is that the potter's hands are replaced by tongs, hammer, anvil, and the other tools of the blacksmith.

It would be wishful thinking to hope that *everyone* could become a good blacksmith. My experience tells me that in this, as in other crafts, everyone has his own degree of skill. One may have great talent, another less, and still another hardly any at all. A simple and good test, which you may apply to yourself, is this: Can you drive a nail into the wall easily? Do you have a natural feel for choosing the correct weight of hammer to pound a sturdy, a slender, or a very thin nail into soft, medium, or hard wood? If you have the combination of dexterity, mental judgment, and feeling to hammer the nail well, it may indicate to what degree you may be successful as a blacksmith.

The following exercises acquaint the beginning student with the techniques and results of hammering hot steel so that in time he also will experience a feel for what can and cannot be done in the forging process.

STRAIGHTENING A ROUND BAR

From the scrap pile choose a ⅜-inch round rod about 15 inches long that is not quite straight and is bent a little.

Start a small, clean fire as described in Chapter 1. Place the bent section of the rod in the center of the fire-mound. With tight-fitting tongs or visegrip pliers, withdraw it when the bent section is *dark yellow hot.* (If the bar is long enough, and the end has remained cool, it can be hand-held.) Place it, humped up, on the anvil face.

With a 2-pound hammer, straighten the rod with gentle taps on the hot curve. Learn to check for accuracy by rolling the rod over the anvil face and watching for spots that are still unaligned. Tap with the hammer on those humped-up areas until the rod rolls on the anvil face in even contact all around.

This simple straightening exercise will give you the feel of the hot steel's malleability, and show you how to strike accurately.

SQUARING A ROUND BAR

Steps 1 through 6 in the illustration show how by a 180-degree tumbling method, a round rod progressively becomes a square one. First one side of the rod is hammered to create a flat face. At the same time the underside of the rod which contacts the anvil will also become a little flat. But because the cold anvil cools the steel on contact, that side will be less malleable. This is why the rod is tumbled over frequently in that heat period. Then the hammering can even out the little differences to maintain the symmetry.

Each time the steel cools beyond a *visible heat glow* (as seen in a semi-dark shop), the steel should be reheated.

squaring the end of a round bar

Assume now that you have succeeded in making two evenly flat faces on the round rod in one heat period (referred to as a "heat"). The critical point is that each time the rod is heated and replaced on the anvil, it must continue to be kept *accurate*. During the next step, the already flat, parallel faces must be kept at an exact 90-degree angle to the anvil face. The hammer blows thus must also be accurate, striking the remaining round sections exactly parallel to the anvil facing. An inaccurate stance, rod position, hammer stroke, or anvil placed at a slant can easily create a parallelogram instead of a square in cross section.

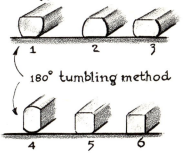
in approx. 2 to 4 heats
180° tumbling method

It is therefore necessary, if this is your first experience, to check quickly the result of the first blows. Look at the end of the rod "head on" to see in what way it may be necessary to adjust the position on the anvil, and what corrective blows must be applied to square the rod properly.

If at first it seems that much is made of little, remember that you must learn corrective actions now in order to apply the gained skill *instantly* later on.

The pride of the good smith is to do a piece of work in a minimum of heats. Endless fussing with steel with many reheatings and ineffective motions indicate the novice's hesitant beginnings. With self-confidence, the faster 90-degree tumbling method, as shown, will soon tempt you to speed up the squaring of a rod end. Quick corrective blows during uninterrupted hammering will prevent the forming of a parallelogram cross section. You will soon improve your skill here, and end up doing perfect square ends.

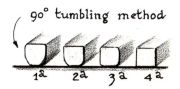
90° tumbling method

Steel can undergo many reheatings before its essential properties are affected, provided it never reaches a *white heat,* or burns. It should not be worked *after* the visible heat glow has disappeared. (It can still be safely *bent*, however, after the steel has become too cool for forging.) If the steel should burn in too hot a fire, you will unmistakably see sparks fly from it looking exactly like sparklers on the Fourth of July. As nothing can be done to restore steel quality when burning has occurred, make sure to *cut off every trace of it,* as follows:

Heat the spot where it is to be cut to yellow hot. Place the cutoff hardy in the anvil hardy hole. Lay the hot steel on the hardy. With a well-aimed hammer blow, the hardy's knife edge will make its first mark on the steel. Replace it in the exact groove for the second blow. (In a quick rolling movement over the hardy you will "feel" that it is in

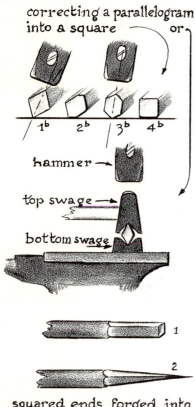

correcting a parallelogram into a square — or —

hammer
top swage
bottom swage

squared ends forged into tapered ends become 1½ to 2 times longer

the correct position.) Just before the piece falls off with the final blow, gently strike it a little *outward* from the hardy edge, and it will be sheared off. This prevents striking the hardy and dulling it or damaging the hammer.

Another way to cut off a section of steel is to place it on the anvil's soft cutoff table using a hold-fast tool which frees both hands for cutting with a chisel head.

If you have ended up with a parallelogram instead of the intended square, correct the error as follows:

If top and bottom swages in the correct size are available, the simplest way is to "push" the hot workpiece into a square between them. Without the swages, however, simply use corrective blows using the hammer and anvil as shown in steps 1b through 4b. But this will reduce the size of the square somewhat.

TAPERING THE END OF A SQUARED ROD

Begin with a squared section of rod. Heat it and place it on the end of the anvil horn. With the flat of the hammer, deliver strong blows, first on one side, then at 90 degrees on the next side, etc., tumbling the rod 90 degrees for each succeeding blow. Deliver these blows as the rod is gradually pulled toward you until the end is reached. This action "pinches" the rod end, as one might pinch a similar section of clay to make it longer. This is *drawing out* the steel.

Using the flat side of the hammer, remove any corrugated hammer marks to make the surface texture summits flush with the valleys. This again pinches the steel, making it longer still. Continue hammering gradually toward the end so that the square cross section is finally shaped into a taper.

The blacksmith's craft is so flexible that there are, as a rule, several ways of doing such things as making a taper. For instance, instead of using the end of the anvil horn, you can use a hardy-type tool with rounded ridge called a *bottom fuller*.

Another way is to hold the rod *away* from yourself, over the anvil face, and hammer with the cross peen, which is easier than with arms positioned over each other (see also Chapter 12). Or tumble the rod in 90-degree sequence using very heavy blows of the hammer-flat without letup at the angle of the taper. The skilled smith will often use this last method for tapering rod ends in sizes up to ½-inch diameter. These very rapid, heavy blows put so much energy in the form of heat *back* into the steel that it stays hot long enough to finish the task in one heat. All that is needed besides skill, in such an operation, is ample muscle and lungs.

SHAPING THE END OF A SQUARE ROD INTO A ROUND CROSS SECTION

The procedure (not illustrated) always works best if the square is first hammered into an octagon. Next the octagon ridges are hammered with rapid gentle blows, one ridge after another, into an approximation of a smooth round surface. (Follow a similar method to make a hexagon bar into a round bar or to shape a square taper into a round taper, etc.)

While doing these first exercises in blacksmithing you will have become aware of one of the most outstanding characteristics of the craft: the *rest period* during reheatings of the steel is in fact an active time. You must plan, deduct, decide, invent, remember, conclude, and keep all "thinking-pistons" firing before the steel has become hot once more. Then the hand and eye must proceed to translate this thinking into the actual forging activity.

4. Upsetting Steel

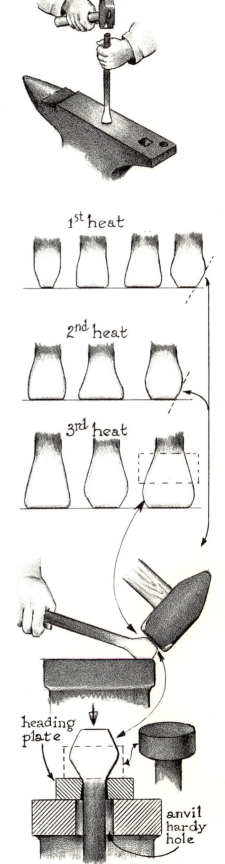

UPSETTING A ROD END TO FORM A BOLT HEAD

Use a ⅜-inch round rod, 17 inches long. Taper ¼ inch of both ends a little, which will tend to keep hammer contact at the exact center of the rod.

Heat 2 inches of one end and hold it down vertically on the anvil. With a 2-pound hammer, strike the cold end with rapid, medium-heavy blows. Aim the blows in the exact vertical direction of the bar to prevent side-glancing and consequent bending of the hot section. If it does begin to bend, *immediately* place it horizontal on the anvil face and straighten it, taking care not to strike too hard, thereby losing the increased thickness you have just gained. *Caution:* Never hit the anvil face with the hammer edge or the peen. Such misdirected blows will leave scars on the anvil that will show as texture on your workpieces.

Hammer the flared-out edge back into a slight taper before returning it to the fire for every next heat. This brings the hot end-face into closer alignment with the center of the rod, and lessens the chance of bending it again during the *next* upsetting action. Apply this corrective treatment throughout the upsetting procedure.

During the third heat, enough volume of steel should be upset to make the size of bolt head desired. If three heats have not accomplished this, however, four or five may be required.

To form the bolt head, place over the hardy hole a heading plate that fits the ⅜-inch rod (see the heading plates illustrated in Chapter 1). Take care that inaccurate blows do not tend to "pull" the malleable mass sideways as you hammer. This danger is real, because you cannot see the resulting rod and head alignment until after the damage may have been done. It is therefore a good practice to look for the slightest sign of eccentricity of the *visible* part you are shaping, making sure it stays aligned with the visible shape of the heading plate. As soon as you notice the head wandering out of line, slant your blows in the opposite direction to put it back in center.

A slight eccentricity between head and shank will not weaken the bolt head's holding strength appreciably. If the head meets the rod with a slight curved edge you can reforge the head back into line.

USE OF THE UPSETTING BLOCK TO FORM A BAR TOOL

The ends of long and heavy bars can be upset without hammers by using the weight of the bar itself as a hammer. Dropping it vertically in a free-fall onto a heavy cast-iron flange upsetting or "stomping" block will in due time compact and thicken the end. Adding *muscle* behind the free-fall makes this upsetting technique very effective and often proves less tiring than the hammer-upsetting of much smaller workpieces.

If sideways bending of the heated end occurs, realign it by hammering it, using the upsetting block as an anvil.

When enough steel volume has been upset on the end of the bar to make a wide, sturdy blade, peen it into the needed width on the anvil with a sledgehammer (see Chapter 2, page 23).

The blade can be *hardened* by heating one inch at the end to a dark cherry red glow and quenching in oil or brine, or it can be tempered by drawing to a straw oxidation color after a brittle quench. If the blade is to be used for cutting trenches in earth without gravel or rocks, it can be tempered brittle hard (as hard as a file). In this case, the cutting angle of the bevel must be somewhat wider to keep the edge from cracking if it should accidentally hit a rock. Under constant use, tools that dig in earth wear better when they are as hard as possible. If you plan to *pry* with the tool, the quenching liquid should be oil, to toughen the blade. For a large heated volume of steel, such as this bar end, the oil container must be deep enough to prevent the oil from becoming too hot and causing a flash fire. Refer to Chapter 6 for further details on tempering steel.

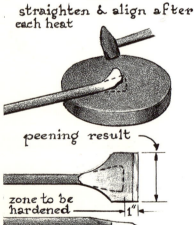

FORGING A HEXAGON BOLT HEAD

To forge a hexagon bolt head freehand, use a previously forged, well-centered, round-headed bolt. Follow steps 1, 2, and 3. In the progressive heats, all angles, if kept correct, will in time result in a sharp-edged hexagon.

If incorrect angles do begin to form, *immediately* place corrective blows as shown. Postponing corrective measures results in the hexagon becoming smaller and smaller.

However, if a small, accurate, but *too-high* hexagon has resulted, it may be forged shorter and wider again by dropping the bolt into the heading plate and hammering the head down to its intended size. This manipulation widens the head as well and may save the project without weakening the bolt to speak of, provided no folds and invisible cracks in the steel have formed.

In any event, final accuracy can be realized by alternately reducing the bolt-head height in the heading plate and after that hammering the hexagon sides on the anvil, until an exact wrench size for the bolt head has been reached.

To thread the bolt shank, clamp the head in the vise and, with a threading die (using lard as cutting agent), cut the thread as shown.

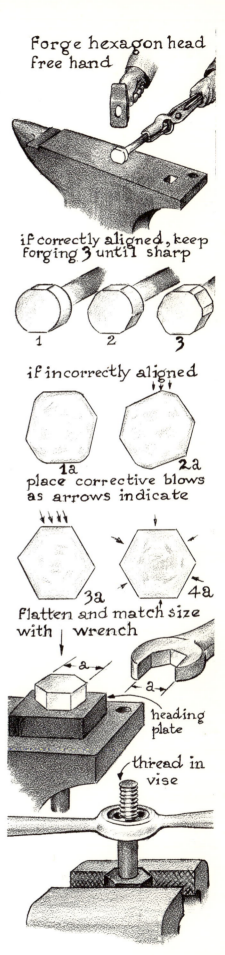

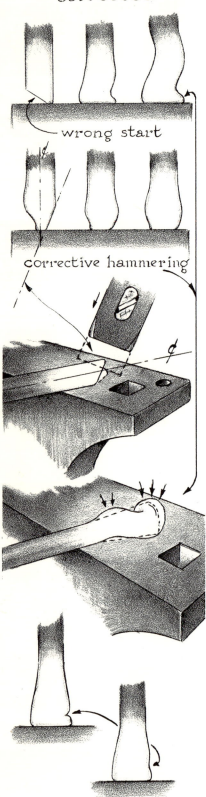

upsetting errors corrected

wrong start

corrective hammering

grind or file every forming fold out before continuing

CORRECTING UPSETTING ERRORS

If the end of a bar is not at an exact right angle to its length, the heated section will unavoidably bend out of line during upsetting. Therefore, it must first be ground or forged into a 90-degree end.

You can meet the difficulty halfway by rounding the rod ends or hammering them into a slight taper. Such ends will receive hammer blows closer to the rod's true center so that even hand-held rods and slightly inaccurate hammer blows will reduce the danger of sideways bending.

Should the hot end bend, it will also start to *fold,* and this must be corrected at once. The fold must be filed or ground out after the end has been straightened and before any further upsetting is resumed. There is no other way to meet this difficulty.

It should be noted that, because of natural human error, all hand-held rods are, to some degree, placed out of line with the anvil. And, of course, hand-hammering also never is as precise as machine-hammering. Therefore, all upsetting actions that rely on hand and eye alone, without the aid of machines, jigs, dies, etc., must constantly be interrupted with corrective hammering before further upsetting can safely be continued.

5. Upsetting with the Aid of an Upsetting Matrix

MAKING AN UPSETTING MATRIX

Often the smith wishes to use tools which serve as "short cuts" when a series of identical articles is to be forged.

The upsetting of steel into bolt heads is a typical operation which uses such a special tool, called a *header-matrix* or *upsetting matrix*. It fits into the hardy hole of the anvil. Illustrations 3 and 3a on page 34 show it in place and in section.

To make a large matrix, a heavy truck axle is good. (Salvaged car axles in all sizes have proven to be excellent material for the making of hammers, swages, fullers, hot punches, as well as matrixes.) A section can be cut, to place in the anvil's 1-inch-square hardy hole for the forming of steel, with a mechanical cutting saw, provided the test with a file (see page 36) shows that the steel is not tempered too hard. High-carbon-steel car axles come in a semi-annealed state and have an inherent resilience that resists breaking. (Only the splines at the end of the axle may have been hardened somewhat to prevent wear by the gear differential movements).

If the car-axle section has a diameter equal to the diagonal of the hardy-hole square, grind the axle to fit the square using the largest grinding wheel.

If you prefer to forge the section into a square as the illustrations show, then the hot section can be driven into the hardy hole as soon as it begins to fit. Whatever does not precisely fit will yield (the steel being malleable) under precise hammer blows. It is now that a 4- to 7-pound sledgehammer should be used (if the anvil weighs 100 pounds or more) to drive the slightly oversized hot metal into the hole to make the best possible fit.

It is good planning to let the square section protrude below the anvil thickness so that the finished matrix can easily be knocked out later. During the making of the matrix, however, when the square section is yellow-hot, it may inadvertently be upset locally should you try to knock it out from below. That is, the end would be made *thicker*, as in riveting, thus locking the matrix into the hardy hole. To avoid this, bevel the end of the square section a little. To be doubly safe, place a ¾-inch bar (smaller than the hardy hole) against the locally beveled and protruding matrix blank, as a driver to knock out the blank.

Assuming all has gone well so far, reheat the piece. Drive it once more into the hardy hole, using a 3½- to 4-pound hammer to upset a little shoulder on the matrix blank where it meets the anvil face. This will prevent the matrix blank from later wedging so tightly into the hardy hole that it might chip the edges of the hole. The matrix must fit snugly without undue strain.

Remove and slowly anneal the piece by placing it in ashes. Since this takes about an hour, working on another project will overcome your impatience.

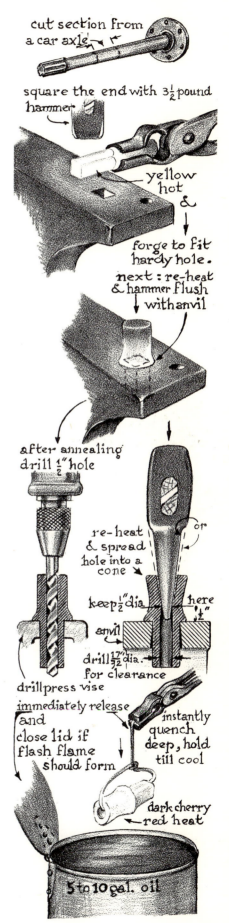

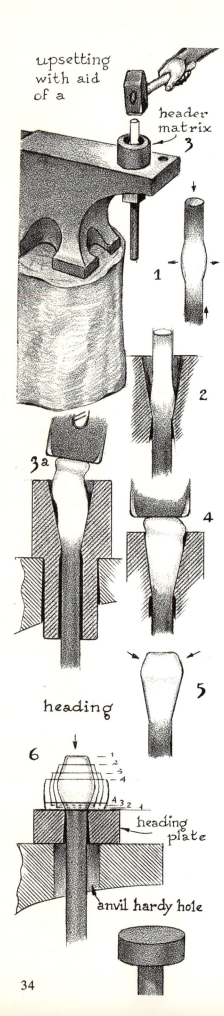

Once it is annealed, test the matrix with the file for hardness to make very sure it is soft enough for drilling.

Place it in the drill vise and drill a hole through the full length of the matrix. Begin with a small drill; the size of the final drill should be the size of the rods you plan to use in the future.

Assume that ½-inch rods are to be used: Clamp the drilled blank upside down in the drill vise, and enlarge the ½-inch hole with a $1/32$-inch oversize drill to a depth which stops just ½ inch *above* the anvil face when the matrix is placed in position in the hardy hole. Now heat in the forge the section of the matrix that extends above the anvil. The shoulder where it touches the anvil should be a dark cherry red while the rest, above it, shows a yellow heat.

Quickly now, insert the taper of a hot punch. With heavy, precise blows, drive it in until it reaches the ½-inch-diameter end of the matrix section (½ inch above the anvil face). It may be necessary to use two or more heats to arrive at this exact position, checking meanwhile with a ½-inch-diameter rod whether it is about to slip through or not, and at what point it does so.

Once you are satisfied that the matrix blank is as the drawing shows, the next and final step is to *harden* it.

String a length of baling wire through the matrix and then heat the whole matrix to a dark cherry red. Holding the wire in tongs as shown, immerse the blank quickly to the deepest part of the 5-gallon bucket of oil. The oil should be at room temperature or a little cooler. The oil bucket should have a hinging lid to snuff out any possible flash fire. Agitating the blank sideways at that depth may promote the process of hardening the outside layer of the steel a little deeper. The inner core will remain a little less hard, just the same, thus preventing it from breaking in use.

UPSETTING STEEL INTO BOLT HEADS WITH AN UPSETTING MATRIX

To upset steel into bolt heads, first heat a ½-inch-diameter rod for about 2½ inches from its end. Then quickly dip the end ½ inch in water before upsetting. The resulting local bulge formed at 2 inches from the rod's end should measure ¼ inch greater than the rod diameter (see illustration 1). Place the matrix in the anvil hardy hole.

Reheat the rod end 2 inches to a light yellow heat, leaving the bulge a dark cherry red. Drop the rod, in this state, into the matrix, where the bulge will be hung up by the cone's narrow throat (see illustration 2). For once, you need not feel too rushed, because you want to let the bulge cool a little on contact with the cold matrix. The purpose is to *lodge* the bulge here, *not* drive it through the narrow throat.

While lodged firmly, the upper light-yellow-hot portion of the rod is very malleable and will respond fully to upsetting, soon filling the cone space (see illustrations 3a and 4).

Forceful hammering thickens the "locked-up" steel, driving it into whatever space within the cone is still not filled. It calls for keen, instant judgment as to how you must redirect the hammer, blow by blow, to avoid too much sideways bending of the rod end.

Illustration 5 shows the end result of the symmetrically upset rod-head. It is now ready for heading with the heading plate (see illustration 6).

Caution: Read carefully how to prevent eccentric wandering of the head during this operation as described in Chapter 4, page 29.

MAKING A CARRIAGE BOLT HEADING PLATE and DECORATIVE BOLT HEADS

A carriage bolt is used to tie wooden members in structures together. These bolts have square cross sections just below the head, so that the corners of the square, pressed into the wood, will "lock" the bolt against turning when the nut is tightened on it.

To make the heading plate as illustrated, use a *square* hot punch, which leaves a square tapered hole. You may use a *round* hot punch to make a round tapered hole first, and follow with the square one. This makes it easier to obtain a more precise placement and lessens the danger of tearing the steel at the punch's exit.

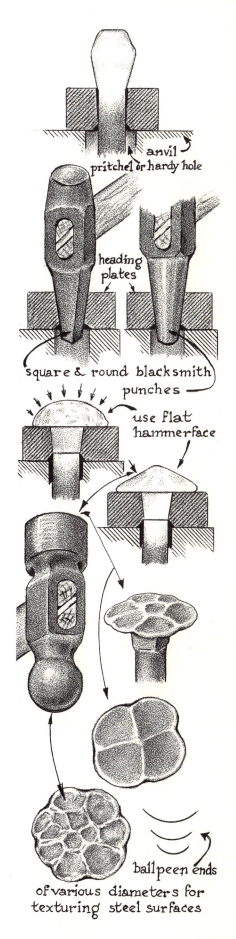

Both square and round-holed heading plates can be used with the small end of the hole either up or down. Used with the small end down, as illustrated, the bolt head is formed after the tapered hole is filled. If the small end is up, then the hot upset steel is driven partly through while "shearing off" some excess steel before the head begins to form. This makes a parallel square section below the bolt head instead of a tapered one. In either case the forging can be knocked out easily.

The shape of the bolt head may be forged as the illustrations show, but the head must be sturdy enough to match the holding strength of the bolt shank. Then it can be decoratively textured to suit your taste. For further details on decorative treatment, see Chapter 9.)

6. How To Temper and Harden High-Carbon Steel

A piece of high-carbon steel can be "chance"-hardened in one quick step; or it can be hardened by controlled tempering for specific hardness in a series of steps.

The blacksmith, as a rule, prefers methods of hardening and tempering which are simpler than those of the specialists who make delicate cutlery, woodcarving tools, or other small articles needing more precise techniques. You must, of course, become familiar with all the ways steel-tempering can be done, and then apply whatever method is most effective for your particular purpose.

In this chapter I present three methods: one, a simple and direct way; and two more elaborate, controlled ways. These include the basic principles applicable to all other methods of tempering.

FIRST METHOD OF TEMPERING

By this method you can harden a cold chisel without tempering.

In the forge fire heat ½ inch of the beveled cutting end of a chisel to a dark cherry red heat glow (as judged in a semi-dark shop, at the moment it is withdrawn from the fire). At this moment, quench the whole tool in water.

This first method is the quickest way of hardening high-carbon steel that can be devised, and most smiths that I have known rarely resort to any other way. In his average daily practice, the smith forges larger, heavier-caliber articles than a specialist in cutlery-making and for most of his work he will use this "one-shot" method.

The File-tip Test for Hardness and Temperability

This test is always a reliable way to test the hardness of steel.

Assume that you have quenched the cold chisel at a *dark cherry red heat glow*. With a sharpened file-tip, press down on the quenched end of the chisel. If it slides off like a needle on glass, the steel is hard enough and can cut mild steel or annealed high-carbon steel.

If the file-tip "grabs" or can "pick" at the surface, it is too soft. In that case, reheat the ½ inch of the chisel end, this time to a medium cherry red heat glow. If it is still not hard enough after quenching, repeat the same procedure once again, this time quenching at light cherry red.

When you are dealing with high-carbon steel, this last should bring correct results. However, if the steel still is not hard, you are then justified in suspecting that it is *mild steel*, lacking the needed 0.2% high-carbon content to make it temperable.

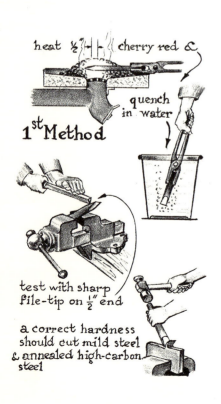

SECOND METHOD OF TEMPERING

This method introduces more elaborate controls, using the temper colors of the oxidation color spectrum as a gauge for degrees of hardness.

In the forge fire, heat 2½ inches of the bevel end of the cold chisel to a dark yellow heat glow (again as judged in a semi-dark shop, at the moment the steel is withdrawn from the fire).

Now hold only 1 inch of the end in the water or brine (in this case *not* in oil because if the hot steel is not *completely* submerged, the oil would flame up). Within a few seconds you will see the visible heat glow of the unquenched part disappear. Only then withdraw the tool.

Immediately rest the chisel, slanted downward, over the anvil's edge, and without loss of time, rub the bevel vigorously with an abrasive stone. This puts a silvery sheen on the steel. (Only on a shiny steel surface will the oxidation color spectrum become clearly visible when held to catch the light.)

The *remaining heat* in the tool now acts as a reserve, spreading gradually, through conductivity, to the bevel end of the chisel. The first color that appears is a *faint straw*, followed by *straw*, *bronze*, *peacock*, *purple*, and finally, *blue*. This color sequence, for all practical purposes, never varies in the average high-carbon steel.

Once the color you want arrives at the cutting edge, arrest the process by quenching the *whole* tool in water. At this point the reserve heat still in the tool will be cooled enough not to brittle-harden it.

In observing the color scale, note that each color must be thought of as a *hardness* indicator.

Caution: If the tool is withdrawn *too soon* after the first 1-inch quench, the reserve heat could still be too great, with the color running *too fast*. In this case, arrest it by a sudden quench. The danger is, however, that this may brittle-harden the too-hot section of reserve heat, causing the chisel to break there during use. To avoid this mistake, never deviate from this rule: Hold the hot tool end 1 inch in the quenching bath *until the visible heat glow has disappeared* before proceeding.

Another mistake is waiting *too long* before withdrawal, since then the reserve heat may not be great enough to make the full color spectrum visible, and it then would be necessary to start all over again.

If the color-run on the bevel should come *slowly to a stop* at the color of your choice, do not quench, but let it continue to cool *slowly*. This has an advantage, particularly when tempering slender tools. The slow cooling creates the least amount of tension, whereas any sudden quench always causes sudden shrinkage, with unavoidable greater tensions in the steel's structure.

Some steels are made to be hardened in *oil only* and others in *water only*. Since a scrap pile of steel will be a mixture of these, it sometimes happens — though rarely — that the faster cooling water quench "cracks" the steel across.

Assuming that all has gone well, you have now learned the basic principles of a more controlled hardening method — the process is called *tempering*. This, combined with the simpler first method, allows the smith, as a rule, all the leeway he needs in hardening and tempering steel.

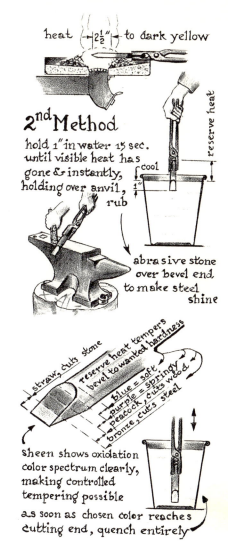

THIRD METHOD OF TEMPERING

This refined method of tempering (not illustrated) is applied to light-caliber forgings, and is the method used by makers of delicate tools and instruments.

Use here a very slender thin cold chisel.

First heat the tool end a light cherry red. With this tool, the *whole tool* is quenched. This leaves the tool brittle-hard where the visible light cherry red was, while the rest of the steel remains softer.

Carefully clean about 1 inch of the brittle tool end on a fine-grit rubber-backed, abrasive disc insert. Polish it to a mirror sheen in order to reveal the oxidation color spectrum prominently. This reduces error to a minimum when judging color.

DRAWING TEMPER COLOR

First, reheat the softer part of the tool over the blue flame of a gas burner, holding the brittle part safely *outside* the heat core of the flame. When the soft part becomes hot enough so that the heat travels outward through the steel by conductivity, you will see (as in the second method of tempering) the oxidation color spectrum appear. This time, however, you have control over the *speed* of the process, manipulating the tool by holding it *in* the flame, or *above* it. Depending on the type of steel composition, oxidation colors can be brilliant or faint. When the color for the specific required hardness reaches the bevel end, *quench the whole tool*.

QUENCHING LIQUIDS

The three most frequently used quenching liquids are water, salt brine, and oil (old motor oil will do), *always used at room temperature*.

In water the steel is cooled quickest; in salt brine, a little slower; in oil, at its slowest.

In all three quenching liquids the hot steel, meeting the identical room temperature, end up with the same *outside* hardness. However, since the boiling points of these liquids vary, the hot steel cools towards its *core* at different rates of speed. The quicker the core is cooled, the harder it becomes. The slower it is cooled, the softer it will be.

A softer core makes the tool tough. The explanation is simply that an *outside hardness* may be kept from breaking under strain when cushioned by an *inside softness*, which combination keeps the tool tough.

In addition it should be recognized that one kind of steel cools faster or slower than another during quenching. Each one thus has its own *coefficient of conductivity* which must be taken into account. It is the combination of these variables which you must be aware of during the tempering procedures.

Effect of Quenching Liquids on Hot Steel

Water boils at 100° C. (212° F.). This cools the *core* relatively fast and the heated chisel bevel will have an almost *uniform hardness;* it will be brittle all the way through after quenching.

Brine boils at a temperature a little higher than water (depending on salt concentration). Therefore the *core* cools a little slower, giving the same *outside* hardness while the core itself, somewhat *softer*, leaves the bevel end a little tougher and less brittle.

Oil boils at about three times the boiling point of water. Therefore the *core*, being cooled slowest, will be *softer still*, while the outside hardness remains the same as tools quenched in water or brine. The oil quench therefore will give the toughest bevel end.

Since it is always difficult to grasp the underlying principles of hardening steel, you should read the foregoing procedures again and again in order to understand clearly what takes place.

Once the three methods of hardening steel have been understood and practiced successfully, you can expand on them in your own way. You will then also begin to recognize how the ingenious methods of smiths in many foreign lands produce many effective results. The various swords, krisses, machetes, etc. that they make not only keep their sharp edges, but their fine blades defy breaking under severe strain.

I once witnessed a Philippine smith bring his bolo knife to an even heat in an elongated charcoal fire, then sink ¼ inch of the curved knife edge into the matching curve of a fresh squash and leave it there to cool. It gave the edge the exact hardness he was after (based upon his judgment as to the proper heat of the steel when sticking it into the squash). The softness in the remainder of the blade graduated from the knife edge to the back. I have owned that very knife all these years, using it for pruning tree branches and for clipping off nail heads in the vise instead of using a cold chisel. The soft steel of the back edge by now has cauliflowered over from hammering on it.

Another time I saw a soft needle-point hardened by heating it in a candle flame. When the very point had a soft glow, it was immediately stuck into a potato!

All over the world we can find endless examples of inventive ways of hardening and tempering steel. All of them, when correctly analyzed, are based on the principles you have now learned to understand.

7. Making a Right-Angle Bend

Making a right-angle bend is like a warming-up exercise. Just as the pianist practices his scales preparatory to giving a concert, with this particular exercise, the smith sharpens his judgment, hand skill, timing, and coordination. In short, his accumulated know-how is brought into play. After these exercises he will be better prepared to undertake the next forging tasks more successfully.

When a rod is clamped in the vise and bent over with a hammer into a right angle, the *inside* will be sharp but the *outside* of the bend will have a rounded curve.

To bend the rod under a right angle and make both inside *and* outside angles sharp is the problem, and one difficult to master. At first this seems easy to do, but the major effort must be to accomplish the task in a minimum number of heats.

Try to visualize what the hammer blows must accomplish. They must *upset* the steel at the bend while not opening the curve further. Use a light hammer with high-velocity blows, pushing the malleable steel together locally while at the same time reducing the *curve* of the bend somewhat. Too heavy a hammer used with driving blows will not increase the upsetting much and tends to open the curve (which you *must* avoid).

To make a right-angle bend, use a ⅜-inch-diameter rod and a light, 1½- to 2-pound hammer and proceed as follows:

Step 1. Heat the rod locally where the right-angle bend must occur. While working on the bend, do not stray from that location. Cool ½ inch of the hot end in water, leaving hot and malleable only the bend location where the hammer blows will strike. Now bend the rod on the anvil horn as illustrated.

Step 2. With a lightweight hammer, use rapid blows in alternate series, hammering first on one end of the rod and next on the other.

Step 3. After sufficient upsetting has resulted, as shown, and the rod at the bend location has become 1½ times thicker, it is time to hammer only the bulge locally at the bend. Place the bend on the anvil, overhanging the edge but well away from it, as illustrated.

Now use a 1-pound hammer, allowing the "mass" of the rod to counter the blows. The mass of the rod can be increased when it is held in well-fitting heavy tongs. Constantly aim to keep the small inside curve of the bend from becoming sharp. At no time must it be "pushed" together into a fold. If that small inside curve becomes a fold at the bend, not much can be done to save the project. As soon as mistakes are observed, *use corrective blows* to prevent further damage.

Step 4. When the outside curve has become sharp, but still is slightly oversize, the whole bend can be safely refined, as the following steps in the illustrations show. Be warned, however, that the almost-finished right-angle bend flush with the anvil's edge may still accidentally be hammered *beyond* that edge. This would drive the overhanging side of the bend down, while flattening the part on the anvil face. All your previous work then is beyond repair.

Examine the common errors closely, as these are shown in the illustrations, so you will be able to avoid mistakes as you work.

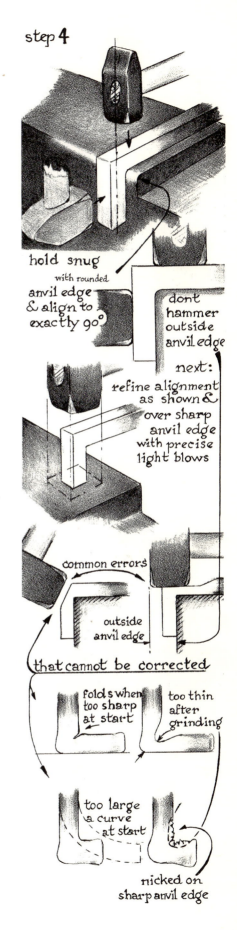

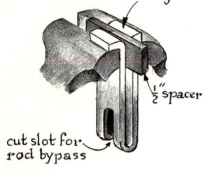

MAKING A JIG TO FORGE A RIGHT-ANGLE BEND

As stock for the jig, choose a ⅜- by 2-inch leaf spring of a car. Cut off a piece 20 inches in length.

Heat 4 inches in the middle and bend it, as shown, clamped between vise jaws with a ½-inch-thick spacer.

Heat the ends of the jig to yellow heat and clamp it once more in the vise with spacer between. Next, quickly hammer the 1½-inch protruding ends outward over the vise jaws, as shown. This results in ⅜- by 2-inch lips with well-rounded edges.

Next, cut a slot at the bend of the jig for the rod bypass. This can be done on the abrasive cutoff wheel, or with drill and hacksaw.

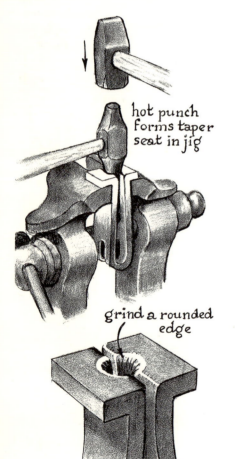

Reheat the ends yellow hot and place the jig once more in the vise. This time, instead of the spacer, insert a ¼- by ¾-inch hot punch, clamp all firmly together and quickly hammer the hot punch down. This forces a tapered depression into each jaw. The depression can be enlarged by squeezing the vise a little tighter at each repeated heating and further hammering down the punch. Thus enlarged, the tapered depression will take a ½-inch-diameter round rod. Round off (grind) the sharp edges at the top of the hole to prevent angle bends from becoming marred during upsetting.

The jig should open just enough to insert the rod and then be tightened firmly in the vise before upsetting.

A RIGHT-ANGLE BEND USING VISE AND JIG

Upsetting using a vise alone, as in illustrations 1a and 2a, also speeds up freehand forming of a right-angle bend, but often leaves scarred surfaces when the hot steel is hammered over the sharp edges of the vise jaws. Using the special jig, as in 1b and 2b, prevents such scarring, and the upsetting is done as fast.

Once enough volume of steel has accumulated around the bend, refine and sharpen the piece as shown in illustrations 3, 4, and 5.

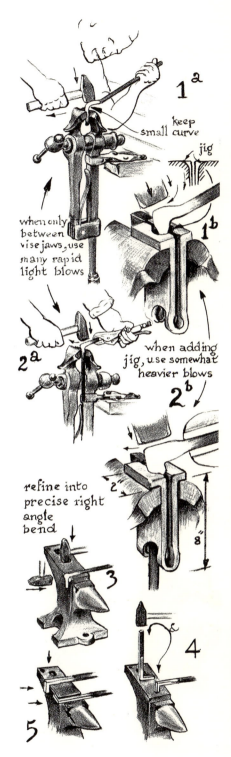

keep small curve

jig

when only between vise jaws, use many rapid light blows

when adding jig, use somewhat heavier blows

refine into precise right angle bend

2"

8"

keep small inside curve until step 4
use vise-grip pliers if tongs fail to hold firmly
3-4-5 sharpens all edges & aligns to 90° angles

MAKING A RIGHT-ANGLE BEND IN A MILD-STEEL ANGLE IRON

Before you begin, make certain that the angle iron is mild steel. Test it with the file tip after a quench (see Chapter 6). Heat the center of the bar to yellow hot and clamp one flange side of the hot section between vise jaws. Hammer it into a precise 90-degree angle with the vise. During the bending the other flange will bulge outward.

Reheat the *bulge only* and quickly quench the flange with the finished right angle halfway in the water, leaving the bulge hot. Immediately place the finished angle over the anvil's 90-degree corner, as shown, with the hot bulge resting on the anvil face. Hold down firmly with visegrip pliers. Using a 1½- to 2-pound hammer, pound the bulge down with rapid, high-velocity blows wherever smaller bulges keep forming.

Even though you have cooled the finished right-angle flange, it will not be rigid enough to resist *some* bending under the strain of flattening the bulge. Therefore, reheat the whole bend and clamp once more in the vise and correct that right angle should it have opened up somewhat. Again, dip-quench that flange only and replace as before on the anvil to further compress and flatten the hot bulge as needed.

When you have arrived at step 4 you will notice a slight curve remaining where the two inside flanges meet. This can be forged into a sharp right angle over the anvil's edge if your plan requires it.

Bending the angle iron over the anvil only, *without* using the vise, will make *both* sides bulge out, but only half as much. One half-size bulge must then be flattened, however, and the other hammered freehand at a 90-degree angle. It can be done, but it is a struggle because of the constant corrective hammering necessary to realign the workpiece.

It is therefore good practice to cool one bulge first in order to keep it rigid while upsetting the hot one. Then alternate the procedure when correcting the other bulge.

MAKING A RIGHT-ANGLE BEND IN A HIGH-CARBON-STEEL ANGLE IRON

If the angle-iron bar is of high-carbon steel, and the vise is used as an aid, the cooling of the exact 90-degree flange should be restricted to a ½ second in-and-out quench in concentrated hot brine instead of water. It is safer against cracking, since in hot brine the steel cools more slowly. This very brief cooling will stiffen that side considerably without brittle-hardening it. Then finish up as in steps 1 through 4.

Note: Do not cool high-carbon steel by a prolonged quenching while making a right-angle bend. If you fear that brittleness has resulted at any given spot, anneal it before proceeding. If a brittle section is a few inches distant from hammer blows during forging, the steel will break off like glass.

8. Some Tools that are Simple to Forge and Temper

A COLD CHISEL

One of the most useful tools to have in a metal-crafts shop, the cold chisel is one of the easiest to forge.

Use as stock a ¾- to 1-inch-diameter high-carbon-steel bar, round, hexagon, octagon, or square.

Heat ¾ inch of the end to a dark yellow glow. Hold it on the anvil face at the angle you want the chisel's bevel to be (a blunt angle for heavy-duty work and the cutting of hard metals; a sharp angle for lighter, delicate work and the cutting of soft metal).

In finishing the tapered cutting end, move it to the anvil's edge (1). This allows the flat face of the hammer to bypass the anvil's face while refining the almost knife-sharp beveled end with light tapping and prevents damage to the anvil should the hammer miss.

Cut off the desired length of the chisel (see use of cutoff hardy, page 16). Next, grind the bevel to a finished state (2), and temper both ends as described in Chapter 6.

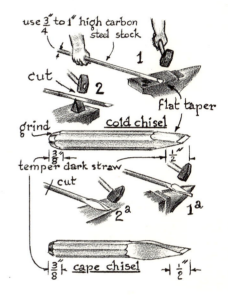

THE CAPE CHISEL

This is actually a very narrow cold chisel. The conventional design allows the cutting edge to be *wider* than the flattened bridge. Therefore, when cutting with this chisel (a key slot in a shaft, for instance), the cutting edge will not bind. The strength of the chisel is great because the flat bridge preceding the cutting edge is wide.

Cape chisels are tempered in the same way as cold chisels.

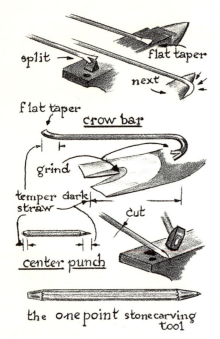

A CROWBAR

Forge the end of a ¾-inch, high-carbon-steel bar to a slender bevel about 1½ inches long.

Reheat and split ¾ inch of this end on the cutoff hardy, and grind the forked end as shown. Reheat again for a length of about 4 inches and bend that section into a curved claw over the anvil horn. The claw end is used to pull nails out of wood, but it can also withstand the maximum strain when used to pry with as well.

The other end of the crowbar is forged in the same way as the cold chisel bit and bent only a little so that it can be used to pry with. Each end is to be drawn to a dark bronze temper color, while the remainder of the bar is kept annealed.

A CENTER PUNCH

Although this tool is easily forged, it can instead be *ground* into its final shape if your motor grinder has a large coarse stone which cuts steel rapidly. Temper as a cold chisel.

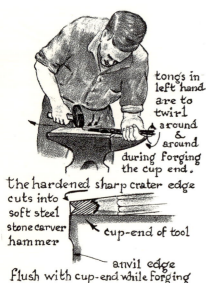

A ONE-POINT STONECARVING TOOL

This tool resembles a center punch and is made similarly. However, the end that is struck with a mild-steel hammer can be forged with a sharp-edged "cup" shape. This sharp, hardened edge bites into the hammer and prevents it from glancing off.

To make the cup-shape, stand at the anvil as shown, using the hammer and tongs as the arrows indicate. Temper both ends as a cold chisel.

9. Decorative Treatment: Rosettes and Wallhooks

DECORATIVE ROSETTES

Decorative rosettes can be made from all sorts of small steel-scrap items. The examples shown here are discs (slugs) of steel like thousands ejected by presses that punch holes in steel plates.

When these slugs are heated *singly* in the forge, they too easily slip down to the fire grate; to retrieve them will upset the fire. Therefore, to heat such small items, put them in a one-pint tin can and place it in the middle of the forge fire, deep enough to have hot coals come up to half the height of the can. All of the slugs will then become equally hot. Do a whole batch at a time if you plan to make several rosettes.

With ⅛-inch thin tongs, pick a hot slug out of the can and place it on the anvil. Heavy pounding with the flat of a 3½-pound hammer thins and flattens it. The slug's diameter is now considerably larger. Place it in the little mound of ashes and cinders *below* the forge to anneal. Treat all hot slugs in this way if they are of high-carbon steel (annealing is not necessary if slugs are mild steel).

After annealing, drill a hole in the center of each disc to fit the thickness of the nail to be used in it.

Next, make a heading die for the texturing of the rosette, as shown. (See also illustrations in Chapter 5).

In this case only the small hole to fit the nail and the larger clearing hole below are drilled.

Place the die in the hardy hole. The heated flat disc first receives the cold nail, which nail in turn is held by a pair of tongs. Together they are placed in the die hole. Once nail and hot disc are in position, use the special large double-ball hammer to deliver well-aimed, forceful blows to shape as well as texture the rosette.

Flip the hammer over in mid-air, using either the small or large ball to give the rosette the desired texture. In this action the nail head becomes embedded in the hot center, automatically seating it to perfection.

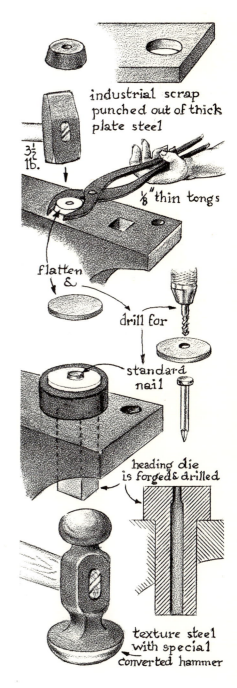

Patination

Prepare the rosettes for patinating with oxidation colors as follows:

With the power sander, gently smooth all textured ridges with a small, flexible, rubber-backed fine-grit paper or cloth disc abrasive. A rubber abrasive will do also. Once the outer ridges shine like a mirror, polish them lightly on the buffer. In this process the "valleys" are hardly touched, so the natural black forging oxidation is kept intact. Finally, clean the rosette with a solvent to remove all wax residue and dry with a clean rag.

To draw the oxidation colors, hold the rosette with the thin tongs and heat it in the hot core of a gas flame, as shown. Soon the first color appears — a light straw yellow. If color moves too fast, hold the rosette higher above the flame. For variety, you can hold *only* the edge in the heat core. It will become dark bronze, then purple, and finally blue. Each rosette then can be variously colored to suit your taste.

Color the textured nail head separately, or simply polish it on the buffer to remove the forge-black. It will then look like a silver button in the darker-colored rosette. Or, if the nail head is patinated a straw yellow, it will shine like gold surrounded by rainbow colors. Such rosettes can be made into drawer pulls and other artifacts.

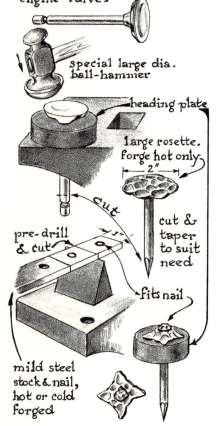

Other Simple Decorative Forgings Made from Scrap Steel

Discarded automobile-engine valves are ideally shaped for making rosette spikes, as the illustrations show.

Although this steel is very hard, it is not temperable or hard enough for making cutting tools. For small decorative items, these valves must be heated to a very hot light-yellow-to-white before this special composition of steel will become malleable enough to yield to heavy hammer blows: We are dealing here with a type of steel that is made to stay *hard* while hot (the engines in which they are used create such heat). This is the reason why you must heat valves to white heat for forging.

Using your own imagination, you can make many other articles from such valves.

Small rosettes are easily made in quantity from rectangular bars and nails. On a 20-inch piece mark off a series of squares and drill a hole in the middle of each one. Cut each square section *almost* through. Heat the first one to yellow heat and slip a cold nail into the hole, then quickly place the assembly flush with the heading plate with the nail in it.

Tear off the cold bar from the heated square and immediately hammer out the rosette to your taste. The nail head automatically becomes textured. Patinate the whole finished piece.

The old-fashioned wood stove lid-lifter made from a bolt is another example of how many ready-shaped items on the scrap pile can be translated into entirely different forged forms.

The same bolt, used inventively, can undergo an entirely different treatment and become a wall bracket for hanging a flower pot or a light fixture — or something else you may need or wish to create.

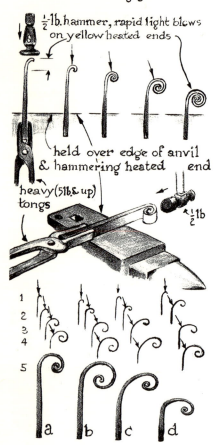

decorative curving of steel without aid of jigs

½ lb. hammer, rapid light blows on yellow heated ends

held over edge of anvil & hammering heated end

heavy (5 lb. & up) tongs

a-b-c-d designs need 1 to 5 heatings to complete. Arrows show direction of hammer blows

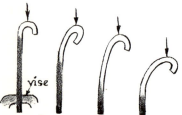

vise

resulting curves vary with heat range, steel size & shape,

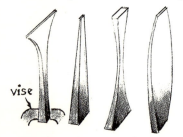

vise

direction of hammer blows & weight of hammer

FREEHAND CURVING OF STEEL

The freehand technique of curving steel is a challenge and a pleasure for the smith. By this means he shapes bars of hot or cold malleable steel into beautiful curves. In contrast, when fixed pattern jigs are used, a machine-like character is injected: the true blacksmith wants to avoid this. Such pre-arranged jigs are used to bend cold, evenly milled steel bars. In the modern gates, grills, and panels sold as "wrought-iron" work, the mechanical quality becomes evident.

No two hand-rendered curves are quite so precisely alike that they are exact duplicates. When bars are heated and tapered at the ends, as shown, they can be curved into a great variety of beautiful designs. In each step, the curving metal is affected by several factors: the weight of the hammer, the direction of the blows, the cross section of the steel where it bends, and how malleable (hot or cold) it is at a particular spot. With freehand skill, then, you can aim for a *combination* of these variables, learning as you work just which will give the most satisfying results. Examine and analyze the illustrations: they are guides to the endless possibilities in this type of workmanship.

A DECORATIVE WALL HOOK

To make a decorative wall hook, cut 6 inches from a round or square ⅜-inch-diameter rod and forge the end into a taper about 3 inches long (step 1).

Heat 1 inch next to the taper. Clamp in the vise between round-edged insets (step 2), bending and upsetting the hot section.

Or, you may use an *upsetting die* (made as illustrated in Chapter 5), which speeds up the shaping of the hook (see drawings 3 and 4) and setting a "head" on top of the tapered end. Hold this head in tongs while drawing out the rod end (step 5).

Further forging of this portion can be varied to suit the taste of the smith, who must now visualize the final product he has in mind.

If the hook end is to be curved, as shown, it calls for gradual widening while at the same time thinning it toward the end. You will start with a tight curve which progressively becomes a more open curve toward the thicker steel (7 and 8).

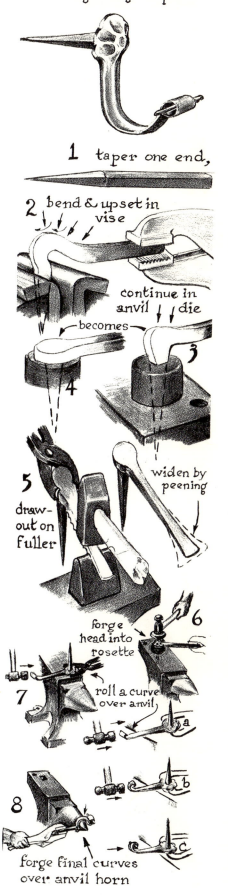

Texture the spike head with the ball peen (6).

The final surface finish can vary from a simple steel brushing and rubbing in of linseed oil to any combination of treatments for patination (see Chapter 9).

10. Hinges

The more skilled you become in blacksmithing, the more you will realize that there are several ways to forge an article. A hinge, in particular, lends itself to inventive design and forging once you have understood how it must work and how to make it.

To describe all the possible types of hinges would fill a book. Therefore, only a few of the most frequently used kinds are offered here as examples. Once you have made these, you will be prepared to meet successfully whatever hinge problem comes your way.

MAKING A HINGE WITHOUT MACHINING

Select a 16-inch-long bar 2½ inches wide by ⅛ inch thick. Heat 3 inches at the end and make a split 2½ inches long with the chisel head (1), cutting it on the soft anvil table (or on the anvil face after covering it with a protective mild-steel jacket). The bar can also be split, as shown (2), on the cutoff hardy.

Reheat yellow hot and spread the branches. Round off the sharp crotch, first on a bottom fuller (3), and further on the anvil horn (4).

After the fork has been opened wide, bend the first branch (5). Bend the second branch parallel to the first. With the aid of a spacer, adjust the two precisely (6). If the thickness, width, and length of the branches become somewhat uneven, refine them freehand on the anvil face. Once more, check for correct spacing between the two.

Heat one branch and curl it freehand (7). Then curl the second branch.

For a temporary hinge pin that will serve for forming, select a piece of round rod ⅜ inch in diameter. Curl both branches completely around it (8). Further fitting is done on the anvil face or over its edge to complete the hinge-pin seating (8) and (9).

Heat the second hinge half and forge it to fit the space between the branches of the first one. Curve it hot over the round rod also (10).

Cut the correct length from the rod for a permanent hinge pin. Rivet a small head on one end to keep it from falling out of the assembled hinge.

Heat both finished hinge halves and assemble with the permanent, headed hinge pin. If the assembly has become somewhat unaligned, the still-hot malleable parts will yield easily to many rapid blows; the self-seeking alignment over the cold pin will "set" the two hinge elements.

While the hinging area is still visibly hot, work the hinge blades back and forth to ensure easy movement.

ORNAMENTAL HINGE DESIGNS

Once the hinge halves have been assembled and work properly, the hinge blades can be forged decoratively to suit the particular areas they must fit (doors, lids, gates, etc.). These hinges are made flat and are bolted onto flat wood.

With visegrip pliers, clamp the hinge blade onto the adjustable steady-rest bolted to the anvil stump. Use a cold-chisel head to cut the hot steel. The soft anvil table allows the chisel to cut clear through the bar as shown. If *mild steel* (not more than 3/16- to ¼-inch thick) is used, it can be held between the bench-vise jaws and cut cold in a *shearing* action with a sturdy cold chisel.

Heat the pointed prongs locally and bend them temporarily sideways so that you can reach them easily with the hammer. Forge the desired curves and decorative pattern you have in mind, using as many heats as you need.

You may have a preconceived design in mind, but often the curves that result *naturally* during bending, peening, and flattening become unexpectedly more attractive, and you should feel free to improvise during the successive steps. The surface textures that also result automatically during the forging of the hinges are attractive in themselves. If you wish to apply added texture on the finished piece, you can deliberately do so using hammers with cross peen *or* ball, or cross peen *and* ball. It is best not to overdo this, as it may then lose its original appeal.

A GATE HINGE

This hinge design can also be used to hang rustic doors and is both strong and practical. The bolt head acts as both bolt part and hinge-bearing socket.

Upsetting the head on a 1-inch-diameter rod will give enough volume to shape the shoulder, the hinge-bearing socket hole, and the decorative head end as well.

After this part has been forged, as illustrated, draw out the remaining section of the rod into a ¾- to ½-inch-diameter bolt shank. Thread it at the end so that, with a nut and washer, it can be used to tie wall and post together also.

Drill the hinge-pin hole, either partly or all the way through the bolt head.

Several greased washers placed underneath the hinge shoulders make smooth bearing surfaces. Adding, or removing, a washer makes it easy to adjust the hanging of the door accurately.

To locate the exact hinge-bolt positions, hang a plumb line along the door post and scribe off the correct heights, one above the other, for drilling the bolt holes.

Adjust the hinge bolts inward or outward to hang the door accurately, relative to the true vertical alignment.

Next, assemble top and bottom hinges, place door in its allotted space, and scribe off on it the exact hinge-bolt locations for the fastening of the door hinges.

I have installed several such hinge arrangements, fitting irregular wood-slab doors to slab posts and walls, and have found them to be about as easy to place as conventional door hinges. If it becomes necessary to remove such a hung door, it is easily accomplished by lifting it in an upward movement out of the bolt head sockets when the door is in *open* position.

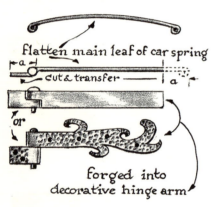

A HINGE MADE FROM A LEAFSPRING

This hinge makes use of the existing calibrated and curled-over hinge ends of the main leafspring of a car.

Heat the leaf and flatten it. Anneal and cut it into two sections, one short and one long, as illustrated. Make a headed hinge pin that slides easily in the leafspring hinge sockets.

After the two arms of the hinges have been forged decoratively, assemble the two parts with the hinge pin. Place in position over door and post and mark off the location of the bolt holes. The fastening bolts, used for such special hinges, can have decorative hammering on the heads as well.

In a variation of the foregoing gate-hinge design, one element is forged to fit *around* the post (see the cross section). Used with a tie bolt, it clamps wall and post together. This is an example of the opportunity you have to design hinges to suit special situations.

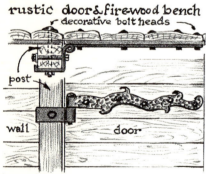

HINGE FOR A WOODBOX BENCH

This practical hinge design is used on a woodbox bench, as illustrated. A long hinge pin, driven into the wood of the bench, secures the hinge arm at the back of the bench to the end of the other hinge arm that binds the box lid together. The opposite hinge of the lid is placed in approximate alignment with the first hinge pin. This box lid acts as a bench seat as well.

11. Hold-Down Tools

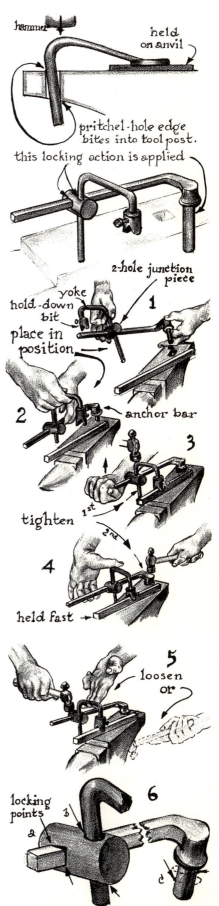

Using a hold-down (or hold-fast) tool to steady a workpiece on the anvil leaves both of the smith's hands free to work. This tool replaces the apprentice assistant who was the standby helper in former times.

Hold-down tools are based on a combination of bending (leverage), friction (locking), and twisting (torsion). A careful analysis of the illustrations will reveal that the fit of the three parts in the hold-fast shown is purposely made *loose*. Once their contact points bite in during the twisting action, the tool and workpiece will be locked together. Therefore, a few light taps of a 1½-pound hammer will hold the workpiece firmly down on the anvil.

HOW TO USE THE HOLD-DOWN TOOL

1. Slip the anchor-bar footing *halfway* into the pritchel hole.
2. Slide the junction piece out of the way from the hot part of the workpiece.
3. Hand-lower the yoke and bit onto the workpiece while driving it down further through the junction piece with a 1½-pound hammer, as much as the tension in the assembly will allow.
4. In this position, the anchor footing in the pritchel hole is rammed down flush with the anvil in a final cinching.

With a little practice these adjustments will take only a few seconds. And now all forging on the workpiece can be carried out during one heat. The smith, with both hands free, can swing a sledge or manipulate a hot punch, a hot chisel, a flatter, a set hammer, and so on.

To loosen the assembly, tap *downward* on the junction piece, or tap *upward* on the anchor footing below the pritchel hole.

The *locking points* in illustration 6 show clearly the principles in the foregoing.

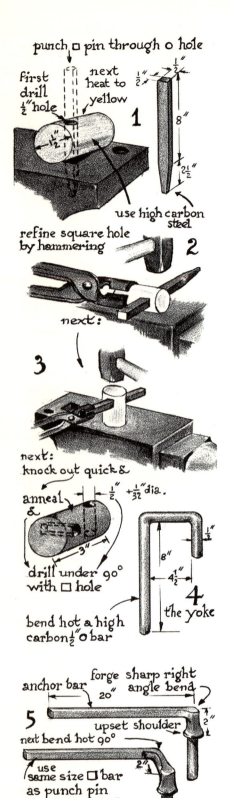

HOW TO MAKE AN ADJUSTABLE HOLD-DOWN TOOL

First prepare a square punch-pin tapered at one end from a piece of high-carbon steel, ½ x ½ x 10½ inches.

Cut off the 3-inch-long junction piece of the hold-down from a salvaged car axle 1½ inches in diameter. Anneal it and make a square hole in it as follows:

Drill a ½-inch-diameter hole through it as shown (1).

Now heat the junction piece yellow hot around the hole (2). Place it over the hardy hole or the pritchel hole of the anvil, and quickly drive the square punch-pin through with a 4-pound hammer. Without a moment's loss, use a 2-pound hammer to pound *around* the inserted pin to bring the hot steel in closer contact with the pin's square sides.

During this action, to prevent the pin from heating up to the point of malleability, hammer it down progressively further through the hot junction piece and, without stopping, refine the fit of the pin into the square hole (3). After the junction piece has lost its forging heat, knock the punch-pin out with one of a smaller size kept handy for this purpose.

At right angles with the square hole, drill a 17/32-inch-diameter round hole, as shown. The ½-inch-diameter yoke bar (4) must fit into it loosely when assembled. The yoke bar is bent hot and left annealed to remain "springy."

To make the anchor bar (5), cut a ½-inch-square cross section high-carbon steel bar 28 inches long. Upset it 5 inches from the end to form a ¾-inch-diameter shoulder. This shoulder functions as a "stop" when the hold-down assembly is hammered down flush with the anvil surface to lock the workpiece in place.

Offset the rest of the square anchor bar 2 inches in order to overhang the anvil edge, well out of the way of most workpieces held fast by the tool.

The hold-down bit can be made with a flat serrated surface *or* with a V slot (as illustrated in drawing 6) to straddle a workpiece. Use a 5/16-inch setscrew to secure it to the yoke end.

All dimensions for the hold-fast tool are approximate, to fit an average 100-pound anvil. You may have to adjust them to the anvil in your shop.

Note that the fit of the square anchor bar into the square hole of the junction piece is purposely a *loose* one.

All three loose fits of the locking points permit easily adjusted tool positions before the assembly is hammered tightly onto the workpiece. It is locked in position by the twisting action of the tools' parts which bite into each other during such twisting. If the hold-down's parts were to fit *precisely,* the locking action could not occur and all would become undone instead of holding the workpiece fast onto the anvil.

12. A Fireplace Poker

fireplace pokers from high-carbon steel springs

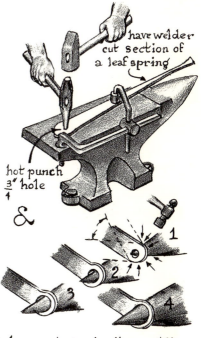

The stock used for this lightweight poker comes from a leafspring of a car. Such a poker can be used easily by those who find many fireplace tools too heavy and unwieldy. Made from this tough steel, it is strong enough to move and pry heavy logs in the fire. The tempered and knife-edged lip is useful for scaling charred wood off burning logs.

Start by making the hole for hanging the poker. With a section of leafspring cut by a welder and held with the hold-fast tool, drive a tapered hot punch through the hot end of the steel, enlarging the hole as much as the taper allows. Enlarge it further by drawing it out over the anvil horn until a thin ring about 2 inches in diameter has been formed (illustrations 1–4). The round ring may be reheated and bent into free-form pattern if you prefer.

Caution: Always stop forging high-carbon steel as soon as its *visible* heat glow disappears. Coming in contact with the cold anvil, the thin, hot, high-carbon steel quickly cools down. This process resembles quenching, leaving the steel brittle. Therefore, you must heat the steel often and for as many heats as you may need to finish the blank. At the same time you must be careful never to overheat the steel because if brought to white heat, the metal will burn.

Next, draw out the handgrip section. Later, two hardwood hand pieces will be fitted to it.

Bend the end lip as shown. If instead you prefer a point and prong at the end, proceed as in the next illustration.

The lip or prong of the poker is tempered a bronze color. The two wood handle sections are riveted to the steel (see procedure for the fireplace shovel, page 84).

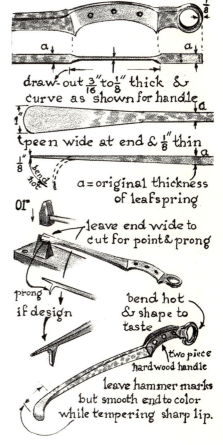

13. Fire Place Tongs

To make a pair of fireplace tongs without hinges, cut a 60-inch length of ⅜- to ½-inch-diameter high-carbon steel stock. At yellow heat, forge the middle 8-inch section, peening it out to a width of 1½ inches. This will leave you about 1/16-inch thickness there.

Smooth and *hollow* the full 8 inches lengthwise at a radius of about 1 inch. This will stiffen its spring-action when in use. This spring-action allows the tongs to open and close, thus replacing the conventional hinge.

Flatten the ends of the rod and forge them spoon-shaped. File teeth along the rims so they will grip charcoal or wood in the fireplace or stove. Flatten the remaining parts of the rod to a 90-degree angle with the middle and end sections. The ⅜-inch-diameter rod should now become approximately ¾ x 5/16 inches. (Or, if you are using ½-inch rod, it should become 1 x 5/16 inches.) This stiffens the tong arms to prevent their bending.

Next, at dark yellow heat, forge the curve of the tong arms as suggested by the illustration. Bend the hot middle section into a 1¼-inch radius hollow swage, using a ball-peen hammer. Then curve the same section progressively until an evenly smooth bend results.

Without a guide strap, the ends of the tongs would spread open too wide. With the slotted guide strap, the jaws are restricted to a certain maximum opening. It also prevents them from bypassing each other when squeezed together. Examine the illustration carefully to make and assemble this strap.

To make the hardwood handles, cut the wood pieces ¼ inch wider than the steel it will attach to. Make in it a slot only as deep as the width of the steel over which it is slipped. Fasten the wood piece in place with three ⅛-inch rivets and countersunk brass washers. Or, if you prefer, make the wooden handle in two pieces as with the shovel, page 84, or the poker handles, page 57.

Lightweight brazier tongs (without hinges) can be made from the wide band steel of the type used to package stacks of lumber or other extra-heavy merchandise for shipping. Literally, miles of this steel are discarded daily at destination points. These tongs should not measure more than 18 inches in length (unless they are to be used to reach for hot coals in a fireplace). The longer they are, the deeper the stiffening grooves must be forged into the arms to prevent them from bending in use.

14. A Spatula Made From a Section of Coil Spring

A thin, flexible spatula is very useful for work in plaster casting, paint mixing, spreading glue, and many other jobs.

Spatulas and similar light-gauge tools can be made from stock of approximately ¼ to 5/16 inch diameter. Good temperable steel of this size can be salvaged from discarded coil springs used in garage doors, garden swings, and many other items. The springs can be handled best when cut into 5-inch sections on the cutoff wheel.

I have invented a practical gadget to unwind these coil sections into straight stock. (See illustration, and also see photograph of this device on page 93). Bring the 5-inch section cut from the spring to a yellow heat in not-too-hot a fire. It is *very important* that during the heating you keep turning this short section over in the fire to make sure the heat is *evenly* spread. Lock a visegrip pliers firmly on ½ inch of the end of the coil, and slip that hot coil over the reel. With one quick and forceful pull, the limp steel will unwind into a straight piece. (If the coil has been heated unevenly, it will unwind as a wavy rod and will have to be straightened later.)

A simpler coil-straightening device can be made by using a ¾- x 10-inch-long well-greased bolt clamped in the vise. Over the bolt, place a section of 1-inch plumbing pipe. The easy turning pipe will function as a reel when a section of hot coil spring is slipped over it and then pulled off.

To make the spatula use ¼-inch-diameter stock from an uncoiled spring.

1. Saw off a 12-inch length and heat 2½ inches at the end. Flatten it to $1/16$-inch thickness with a 4-pound hammer, using rapid, forceful, and accurate blows. Do it in *one heat* if possible.

2 and 3. Grind the forged blade to the shape you want. Clean-grind each side but keep the blade to that $1/16$-inch *even thickness*.

4. Reheat the blade to dark cherry red, then, holding it vertically, quench it in oil. If the blade is an even $1/16$-inch thick, it should emerge without warping. If it is irregular in thickness, or is paper thin, warping may result, requiring reheating and realigning. This time grind very carefully to maintain an even thickness. Measure for accuracy with the calipers if there is any doubt, before brittle-quenching once more. Now the blade should emerge from the quench perfectly aligned and brittle-hard.

Illustrations 5 and 6 show the blade being ground thinner. Try not to lose the brittleness through overheating. Hold a finger lightly on the blade while grinding; if it becomes too hot to touch, interrupt grinding momentarily, holding the blade $1/16$ inch from the stone to allow it to cool in the air thrown off by the stone as it revolves. Repeat this finger-testing and cooling method as often as necessary until blade is as thin as you want it. (This is one time you could wish to have an old-fashioned watered grindstone moving at slow speed. Such a stone will never heat up the steel.)

Once the blade is thin enough (experience will tell you later how flexible you can make it), it can be tempered as shown in illustrations 7, 8, and 9.

15. A Door Latch

This door latch calls for the forging of three keepers that are riveted onto the base plates, and a latch bolt which slides through the keepers.

To make a keeper without a jig is possible, but cumbersome. With a jig, several of them can be made quickly. Two types of jigs are described here. The third method described is a compromise.

Keepers, in one shape or another, are required for many different projects. Therefore, the time taken to make these jigs for them is not wasted, since they are welcome accessories for the shop.

FIRST METHOD: A SLOTTED JIG

Use a section of steel salvaged from a leafspring of a heavy truck, approximately 3/8 inch thick, 3 inches wide, and 18 inches long. Straighten and anneal the spring.

With the abrasive cutoff wheel, make two lengthwise slots in the bar, leaving a middle strip as shown. (The thickness of the keeper stock must be equal to the thickness of the cutoff wheel that cuts the slots.) This section is bent out (hot or cold) to make space for the heated keeper to be inserted under it.

The keepers are partially forged into a decorative shape. Hold the jig down on the anvil and insert the yellow-hot keeper. Immediately press down the set hammer on the center of the jig above the keeper and deliver a hard blow with a 4-pound hammer. This forces the keeper's center uprights and sides into its final shape in one stroke.

The jig's inherent spring-steel resilience makes it unnecessary to harden or temper its "working" end. The only possible trouble it might give is if the stock for the keeper is too thick, which could force the jig's sides outward.

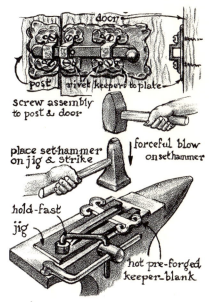

1st method

SECOND METHOD: A SPRING-ACTION DIE SET

In this method a separate small die (a) is cut out with a saw from a solid, high-carbon steel bar. Or you may forge it into the desired shape. File it to the exact size of the latch bolt and rivet it onto the end of a leafspring of a car. As a rule these springs measure about 2½ to 3 inches wide and ¼ to 5/16 inch thick. Cut the jig about 30 inches long.

At the other end of the spring make a slot wide enough to leave room for the thickness of the keeper on each side of the die's boss. The 6-inch middle section of the leafspring, prepared in this way, is heated about 4 inches in its center and bent over, as shown.

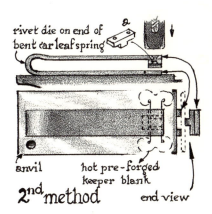

2nd method   end view

This die set can be placed free on the anvil face when you are using a set hammer. Press the set hammer down on the end of the jig, forcing the die down onto the hot keeper blank, before striking it with a 4-pound hammer.

If you do not want to use the set hammer, clamp the hot keeper between the jaws of the jig as if the jig were a pair of tongs, and place it squarely over the middle of the anvil. Hammer the die ends together with the flat face of a 4-pound hammer.

THIRD METHOD: A VISE AND A BAR

Open the vise jaws to the width of the bolt plus *twice* the thickness of the keeper stock. Use a bar as thick as the bolt to force the keeper blank down onto a prop below. Once the hot keeper is forced down in this way, remove and reheat it. Clamp the now folded keeper firmly on the bar in the vise to the depth of the keeper. Both your hands are now free to spread the two ends of the keeper outward with a chisel wedge. Hammer the ends down flush with the top of the vise jaws.

An alternate method is to replace the bar used in the above description with the same stock as that used for making the latch bolt. Place that bar over the hot keeper which straddles the open vise jaws, and simply hammer it down. This action automatically results in the correct final shape of the finished keeper.

Many other methods are possible, depending on your available equipment and your ingenuity. The guidelines to improvisation should be to consider *many* methods instead of only the suggested ones.

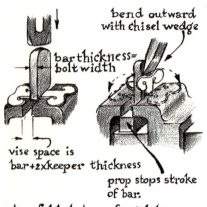

bar folds hot pre-forged keeper-blanks between vise-jaws
3rd method

MAKING THE BUTTON ON THE DOOR-LATCH BOLT

Using a bar that fits the size of the keeper, upset it at one end to get as much volume as possible. Several heats will be necessary to gain enough material to commence the shaping of the spherical button over the jig and the horn. Use a fairly light hammer (½ to 2 pounds), alternating the strokes between the flat face and ball-peen ends.

The knob end of the bolt may be curved outward to suit your taste. Keep in mind that it should be easy to operate.

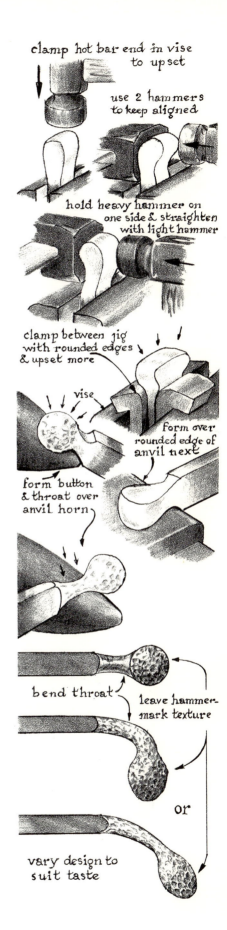

16. Making an Offset Bend in a Bar

Often offsets must be forged in special hinges, door-bolt receptacles, wall hangers, straps that join boards of different thickness, and so on. To forge an offset bend, proceed as follows. Heat the portion of the bar to be offset to yellow hot and place the bar on the cutoff table so that portion overhangs the table. Fasten the cold part to the anvil with a hold-down tool.

Place a set hammer or a flatter on the hot overhanging part and, using a 4-pound hammer, strike it with one or two heavy blows. This offsets that portion accurately and simply. To increase or decrease the amount of offset or jog, build up the anvil face or the cutoff table with plates of various thickness.

Another method of offsetting is to use a jig, as illustrated, which allows you to shape the piece without using the anvil. Clamp the jig in the vise. Hold the cold section of the bar with tongs and place the hot part in the jig slot. Hammer successively each side of the offset 90 degrees, flush against the jig's side, to complete the offset.

Next, reheat and true it up by squeezing the whole assembly between the jaws of the vise (assuming your vise is heavy and strong enough to exert the needed pressure).

Still another way of offsetting is simply to place the combined jig and heated bar, held together with visegrip pliers, on the anvil face, and hammer all down into proper alignment.

Bending an offset in a rod or bar can also be quickly and easily done in specially made bending forks placed in the anvil's hardy hole (see illustration). These forks are designed in a variety of shapes to solve a wide range of bending problems. Heated sections of rods and bars held in the appropriate fork can easily be twisted in this system. But your anvil must be firmly bolted down on a well-anchored wood stump or strong base and the fork must fit snugly in the hardy hole. Additional trueing-up is usually needed with hammer and anvil or in vise jaws.

17. Blacksmiths' Tongs

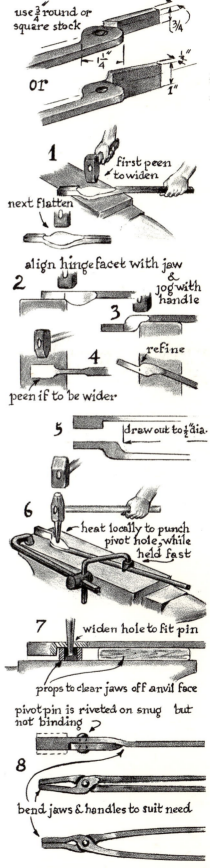

The modern smith faces a permanent puzzle when he makes a pair of tongs without resorting to welding. In tongs the thick, strong jaws and hinge must be combined with handles that are relatively thin to keep the weight of the tongs down without losing the tool's strength. In selecting stock for this tool, therefore, you will have to compromise and use an in-between size to avoid having to weld thin handles on too heavy jaws (as old-timers often did).

To make a pair of blacksmiths' tongs, use ¾-inch square or round stock. It can be either mild or high-carbon steel. For these symmetrical tongs, each half is to be forged *identical* in shape to the other. Illustrations 1 through 5 show how to ready each half.

The hinge pin should preferably be ⅜ inch in diameter for the average (medium-sized) tongs. The hinge-pin hole is hot-punched. Since the area around the hinge-pin hole is subjected to great strain, and must be sturdy, try to leave about ½ inch of steel around the pin. The total hinge area for such tongs then would be approximately 1¼ inches in diameter.

Heat the hinge area and place it over the hardy hole. Secure it with a hold-fast. Punch the pivot hole through with the ¼-inch hot punch (illustration 6).

Reheat and, with the same punch, widen the hole from the other side over a section of plumbing pipe (illustration 7). This does two things. The bulge created when the hole was driven through is bent back in place, while at the same time the hot punch tapers this end of the hole and widens it to ⅜ inch. When assembled, the riveted hinge-pin then fills the cone portion, with a holding action. This, in addition to the rivet heads on the pin, tends to prevent a wobble in the tongs at the least strain. (I venture to say that wobbly, loose hinges are the rule in most blacksmiths' shops, caused by undersized, ill-fitting, and weak hinges.)

When the parts are permanently assembled, heat only the jaws in the fire, without taking the tongs apart. Each jaw can then be bent or reshaped as needed to fit any workpiece for which you may not have special tongs.

blacksmith tongs
most useful jaw types

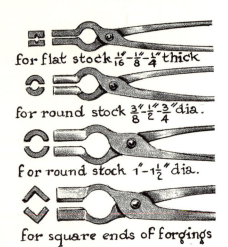

for flat stock 1/16"-1/8"-1/4" thick

for round stock 3/8"-1/2"-3/4" dia.

for round stock 1"-1 1/2" dia.

for square ends of forgings

to hold thin flat discs

to hold parts with hole in end

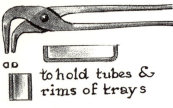

to hold tubes & rims of trays

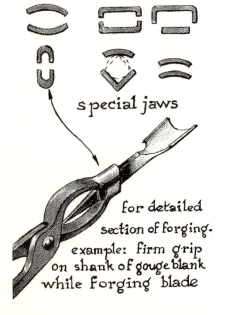

special jaws

for detailed section of forging. example: firm grip on shank of gouge blank while forging blade

Specific workpieces demand different jaw shapes in the tongs used. The shapes shown here simply aim to give an idea of the kinds of stock different tongs are suitable to hold. For instance, the woodcarving-gouge blank shown required the narrow-slotted tongs to match the gouge's upright shank. These tongs can, of course, be used for other things as well.

It is always possible to reforge an old pair of tongs whenever a new project demands a new shape. But whether tongs are new or reforged, it is greatly to your advantage to increase the range of tong shapes and sizes in your collection.

18. Making Milling Cutters, Augers, and Drills

Small hand-forged items in need of some machining can be speedily and accurately refined and finished without benefit of a true metal-turning lathe if you have a good power drill press. The makeshift methods offered here will be completely sufficient for most "precision" work around the modern blacksmith's shop.

By resorting to positioning by sighting, you can, as a rule, get accurate results without the often laborious instrument-measurings in a "make-ready" procedure. Once understood, you can gain a new independence simply by making use of your body's built-in measuring instruments: the eyes (sighting) and the fingers (calipers, etc.), combined with judgment, know-how, and inventiveness.

A MILLING CUTTER

First, accurately forge a 3-inch-long round-headed bolt from ½-inch-diameter round high-carbon steel rod, as described in Chapter 4.

Clamp it in the drill-press chuck and adjust the spindle speed to about 3000 rpm.

Next, tightly clamp, upside down and exactly vertical, a ¼-inch high-speed steel drill in the drill-press vise. The drill must be perfectly sharpened for this function, and should only protrude above the vise jaws ½ inch. Align the drill point by sighting it with the drill-spindle center, after which, with a C clamp, secure the drill vise onto the locked drill-press table.

Switch on the motor and lower the bolt head so that it barely touches the sharp drill point. This is done to clean the contact spot between the bolt head and drill. It "shaves" it evenly, ready to begin the hole to be drilled.

At this point, loosen the C clamp a little to let the vise follow the central pull on the drill point. Then, as you lower the bolt head, the drill will begin to "bite" into the steel. Automatically it will be drawn to dead center of the bolt's rotation.

Your previous sighting of the drill and chuck spindle most likely is now off very slightly (but, as a rule, not more than $1/32$ of an inch). It is this slight inaccuracy that allows the drill to seek a center position automatically, pulling the following vise with it. As you hold the height of the bolt-head position steady for 30 seconds at about ⅛-inch drill penetration, you will see that initial slight movement of the drill point come to a stop. Lock the vise with the C clamp on the drill-press table, and switch off the motor.

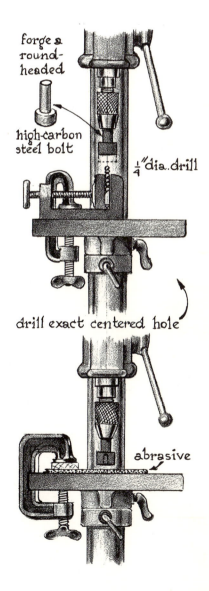

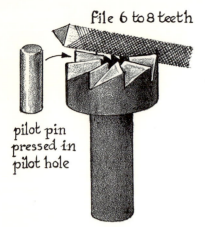

file 6 to 8 teeth

pilot pin pressed in pilot hole

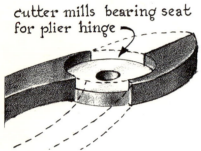

cutter mills bearing seat for plier hinge

Now reduce speed to about 1000 rpm or less, and drill the pilot hole at that speed until the bolt head comes flush with the vise jaws. Raise the bolt head, stop the motor, and remove the drill, but keep the vise tightly clamped on the drill-press table.

Again lower the bolt head until it rests flush with the vise jaws. This time clamp a flat file tight in the vise, so its sharpened, squared-edge end is vertical and touching the rim of bolt head. This file end will now act as a cutter to reduce the bolt head to proper size and to accurate alignment with the pilot hole and bolt shank.

With drill spindle raised, switch on motor and adjust to 1000 rpm or less. Pump the bolt head up and down along the file cutting edge. When you are satisfied that all excess steel has been removed, with the file end at this position you may still judge that more has to be trimmed off. By simply tapping with a 1-pound hammer on the side of the vise, it will yield just enough for you to see a bit more steel being cut off the bolt head. As soon as it is clean, measure its diameter for size.

Next, replace the vise with a flat abrasive stone clamped on the drill-press table with a little wooden cleat as a cushioning block. This time adjust spindle speed to its highest and switch on the motor. Gently lower the bolt head onto the abrasive. This will grind its plane at 90 degrees to its length exactly and smoothly.

This finishes the machining of the cutter blank. Now remove and clamp it, head up, between the jaws of the workbench vise, in order to file the 6 to 8 teeth. Temper to a dark bronze color.

The illustration shows the end result, with the ¼-inch-diameter pilot pin ready to be pressed into the cutter's central hole. Should the pin fit too loosely, dent the portion to be inserted with the hammer peen so that it can be forced in with a wooden mallet.

You now have a milling cutter, a very useful tool. It will prove to be one of your most valuable tools for seating hinge-joint surfaces for pliers, shears, tinsnips, etc.

With the pilot pin removed, such a cutter can become a *router* (provided each cutting tooth is also sharpened on its upright side). Steel sections then can be surfaced and deepened that must be exact and smooth.

AUGERS

Forge the auger blank (illustration 1) and anneal it. Grind it smooth and of an even thickness, with sharp 90-degree edges and sides.

If it is mild steel, twist it cold for an even screw pitch. If it is high-carbon steel, twist it when evenly hot. If it is not heated *evenly,* an irregular screw pitch will result and you will have to start over again. If the alignment should be incorrect, place the still-hot blank on a wood stump and align it with a wooden mallet. If done well, it will not distort the screw shape.

Bend and file the end of the auger as in illustrations 2 and 3. The leading cutting points must be razor-sharp and on the auger's exact diameter, plus 1/64 inch over. *Only the cutting end of the auger is to be tempered and drawn a peacock to bronze color.* (If you make the auger of mild steel, the cutting end must be case-hardened.)

WOOD DRILLS

The simplest, but most effective wood-drill bit can be forged and tempered in a short time (illustration 4). For extra-wide cutting blades, upset the stock first and peen it wide.

Temper wood-cutting edges between peacock and bronze color when the bit is made of high-carbon steel. If made of mild steel, it must be case-hardened.

DRILLS FOR CUTTING STEEL

The difference between this steel drilling bit (illustration 5) and the above (4) is that it must have a thicker blade and a cylindrical pilot lead. This pilot must be filed precisely to fit into a predrilled hole in a steel workpiece to create an accurate seating (as in the making of the hinge-bearing surface of pliers, page 80).

If the stock used is high-carbon steel, temper the last ¼ inch of the blade at the cutting edge a bronze to dark straw. The rest of the blade may be drawn purple to blue.

If the stock used is mild steel, case-harden the bit locally.

All kinds of makeshift wood drills can be made from various sizes of nails (illustration 6). (Remember that nails are mild steel. Such drills, if dull, will heat up and "burn" themselves through wood.) It is perhaps a practice which is frowned upon, but if you are in a hurry and if no great accuracy is required, I see nothing against it.

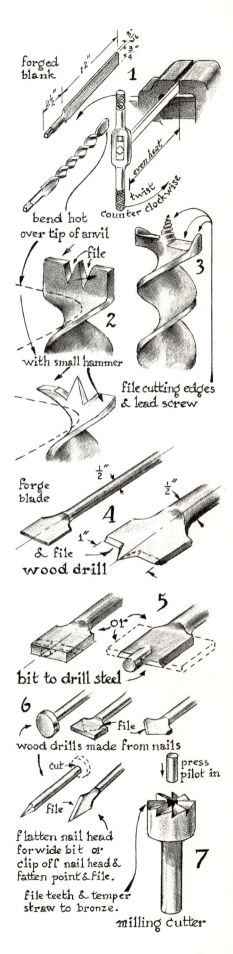

69

19. Stonecarving Tools

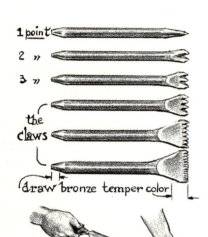

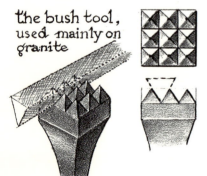

The most commonly used stonecarving tools are simple tools, little changed in design from earliest times. As a rule, stonecarving tools measure about 8 to 10 inches long, and ⅜ to ¾ inch thick. All are made from high-carbon steel.

ONE-POINT STONECARVING TOOL

The one-point tool is made and tempered in the same way as a center punch (Chapter 8) except that the end that is struck by the hammer has a small cup-shaped crater with a hardened knife-sharp rim. A mild-steel hammer, striking this end, will never glance off because the cup "bites" into its face.

TWO-POINT, THREE-POINT, AND THE CLAWS

The teeth are filed into the tapered blade. To temper, heat ¾ inch of the blade end and, after brittle-quenching, put a sheen on the blade with an abrasive. Draw to bronze color over gas flame.

BUSH TOOLS

These tools generally have nine points only, when used for shaping the first forms in stone too hard for the one-point. Others can be made with many very fine teeth for creating smoother textures on the stone's final surface. Held and struck at a 90-degree angle to the stone, it crushes the hard surface. The end of the bush tool that is struck with the hammer is slightly crowned and then hardened. These tools are especially effective when used with air hammers. A bush hammer has a face with nine points and functions as bush tool and hammer combined.

DRIFTS

These tapered round rods are used for splitting stone. A series of holes is drilled in the stone with star-drills or carbide-tipped drills and the tapered drifts are wedged into them. One after the other they are driven gradually a little deeper until they exert the total force necessary to split the stone. They are made of high-carbon steel left in its annealed state.

CLEAVING CHISEL

This stone-splitting tool is made by upsetting a ¾-inch round rod, then using the cross-peen hammer to widen it. It can also be made by beginning with a much thicker (1¼-inch-diameter) bar, upsetting and widening one end and drawing out the other.

The last ¾ inch of the wide blade is tempered to a bronze color. The other end may be hardened and somewhat crowned to keep hammer contact at the tool's center.

drift
highcarbon steel left annealed

wedge pin to drive in pre-drilled hole(s) to split stone

draw temper color bronze — ¾"—

cleaving chisel to crack off segments along precut groove.

20. Wrenches

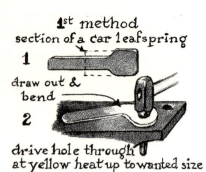
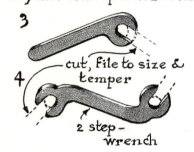
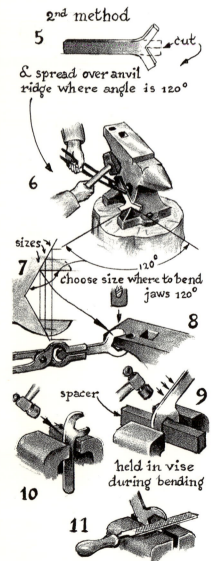

You will sometimes find yourself tempted to whip out a needed, easy-to-make tool that you have lost or mislaid. I have often made a duplicate wrench, screwdriver, hammer, garden tool, rather than spend the time searching for it. The happy result is that wherever I happen to be working — in the shop, studio, house, or garden — there is always a spare one nearby.

OPEN WRENCHES

First Method

An open wrench is easily made. The blank is cut from a salvaged leafspring of a car.

With a hot punch, make a hole and enlarge it to the size you need (illustrations 1 and 2).

Cut away excess and file to exact size (3). Temper to purple color.

To make a two-step open wrench (4), simply forge a duplicate at the other end, and bend them in the opposite direction to each other. The ends are cut open hot with chisel head and hammer, *or* they can be cut by sawing them cold after annealing.

Second Method

As shown in illustrations 5 and 6, cut the end of the hot piece and spread it open over the anvil base where the angle measures approximately 120 degrees. (It is practical to use any part of the anvil which lends itself to the forming and bending of steel. I frequently use the hollows between the horn and base, or between the two anvil footings, to shape articles matching the needed curves.)

Study the *diagram* (7) and choose the size at which to bend the jaws to a 120-degree angle. Shown are the three locations that correspond with three wrench sizes (8). Bend one jaw while holding the wrench horizontally on the anvil's edge. Repeat with the opposite jaw. Hammer it down flush with the anvil facing.

If the wrench head must have a jog with its handle, bend the handle hot just *below* the jaws (9 and 10.) A *spacer* is handy to arrive at an exact size, with further refining by filing the annealed jaws (11).

After brittle-quenching in oil, draw temper color to bronze or purple.

This second method works well to make an *extra-wide* wrench; for example, one that fits the hexagon pipe-locking ring on a plumber's gooseneck trap.

BOX WRENCHES

Draw out the center section cut from a piece of spring steel over the anvil horn or a snub-nosed hardy (illustration 1). When the desired length for the wrench has been reached, punch a hole in each end large enough to receive a hexagon-sided hot punch made especially to convert round holes to hexagonal ones. (You can make this punch by grinding it from a high-carbon steel bar.) Use it with or without a handle. This hot punch is tapered and graduated for size so that it can be driven through prepared smaller holes up to the marked size you need (illustration 2).

Knock out the punch and reheat the wrench head.

Next, use a case-hardened bolt head (4) instead of the punch. It too is somewhat tapered at its end to act as a starter, which can seek a proper seating with the prepared, but slightly undersized hexagon in the box-wrench or head.

If the bolt is long enough, it can be hand-held. Place the hot end of the wrench on a section of pipe which has an opening large enough for the bolt head to be driven through. This "calibrates" the wrench to a perfect fit for that bolt size.

Temper the wrench heads peacock to purple, leaving the center bar annealed.

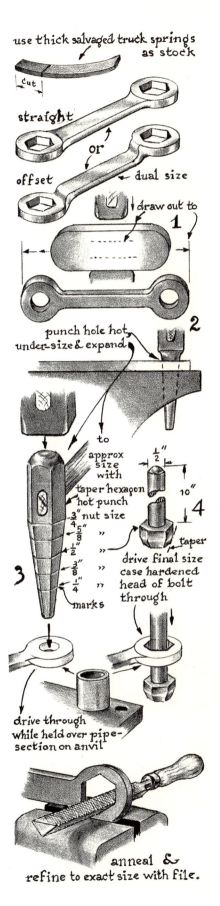

21. Accessory Forging Tools

Worn hammers made of good steel may be saved and made usable. Such a hammer, if you find no deep cracks anywhere, can be forged into any specially shaped hammer you may need.

Most of the double-ball hammers that I have made to form the curves of gouge blades are converted from secondhand hammer heads.

Hammer a temporary steel plug into the hammer-stem hole (illustration 1). This allows you to squeeze the hammer (heated yellow hot) between the vise jaws without collapsing the thin-walled middle section. A steel prop, placed below it and resting on the vise bar, takes up the blows as you reshape the hot hammer head and relieves the stress on the vise jaws. At the same time, the vise bar below also is protected by the prop (2).

Once the ball end is shaped, heat the other end, and convert it also to the shape you need. These hammer shapes should match the curves of swages (3).

Swages can be modeled from secondhand ones (if you are lucky and can find them). But you can also forge new ones from sections of very-large-diameter salvaged truck axles, in shapes as shown on page 16).

Having a choice of special hammer shapes, as shown in illustrations 4 through 7, is a great advantage when curving steel, or when decorative texturing of surfaces needs to be done.

Illustration 8 shows a forming swage used to forge a reinforcing rib on thin blades. This rib down the center of the blade reinforces a light tool to make it strong.

Bicks (9) resemble anvil horns. They are indispensable when projects call for bending tubular parts, cone-shaped sheet metal, and many other jobs that cannot be done on the anvil horn if this part of the anvil is too large. Bicks can be of several sizes, shapes, and lengths, and are quite easy to make. From square stock that fits the hardy hole, forge them into cone-shapes and then bend. Temper them peacock to purple color.

22. Woodcarving Gouges

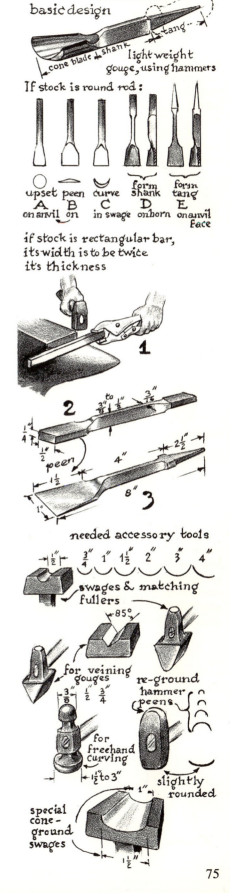

A CONE-SHAPED GOUGE

The advantage of the cone-shaped gouge blade shown here is that this tool will not bind when cutting deep curves in wood, whereas the conventional cylindrical blade will.*

The steel that I have found to be quite satisfactory for the forging of gouges is the high-carbon round or square stock salvaged from coil springs that have been cut and straightened (see Chapter 20).

Follow the steps in illustrations A, B, C, D, and E to make the cone-shaped blades. You will find that the main difficulty in the forging of tool blanks is to keep blade, shank, and tang in precise alignment.

After the blank is formed, refine it by hand-filing and motor-grinding with coarse- and fine-grit wheels, grinding points, and the rubber honing wheel. Finally, polish it with the motor buffer, temper peacock to bronze, and attach the wooden handle.

Instead of using coil springs as stock, you will find the work somewhat simplified if your scrap pile has some high-carbon steel bars, ¼ x ½ inch or ⅜ x ¾ inch. Illustrations 1, 2, and 3 show clearly the advantages of using stock with dimensions already close to those of the planned workpiece: this makes the forging easier and less time-consuming.

Proceed as follows:

1. Forge the shank to ³⁄₁₆ x ½ x 4 inches.

2. Peen the blade to 1 inch in *width* and at exactly 90 degrees to the shank. On the anvil's face, "set" the blade flush with the shank, so that the bottoms of blade and shank form a *straight line*.

3. Hold the blade in tongs or visegrip pliers and forge the tang, leaving a shoulder between shank and tang. This shoulder is made to rest on the ferrule and washer when the tool is assembled with its wooden handle.

In the making of conical blades for gouges of various sizes, you will find that a wide variety of bottom swages and top fullers will make your work easier, as will a choice of specially shaped hammers that fit the swages. However, standard swages and fullers can be used during preliminary steps, the blade being finished freehand after that.

---

*I have discussed the cone design in my book *The Making of Tools*, Van Nostrand Reinhold, 1973.

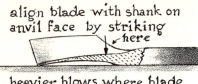

align blade with shank on anvil face by striking here

heavier blows where blade is thickest, until bottom of shank & blade are straight

Assume that you have forged the blank with a flat blade. Place this blade in the nearest-size swage groove and gently peen it down without marring its smooth surface. You will notice that during this forming of the blade the thicker part becomes humped up relative to the shank, because it resists the force of the hammer blows. It is this thicker part which now must be hammered down to restore the alignment with the shank.

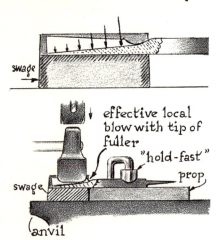

swage

effective local blow with tip of fuller
"hold-fast"
prop
swage
anvil

If you have a hold-fast tool, your alignment task is simplified, as the illustration shows.

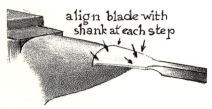

align blade with shank at each step

close or open blade curve when needed during refining over horn

Next, form the cone shape of the blade by opening or closing the curves over the horn and in the swage, until, as you progress, the exact curve and alignment have been reached.

The conical-blade gouge blank is now ready for refining.

important steps in forging conical blades of gouges in cylindrically ground swage grooves.

Shaping the Blade with a Standard Swage

If you do not have a special cone-grooved swage, you can use a standard cylindrically shaped one by employing the special techniques illustrated here.

Note particularly how first one side of the tool is placed parallel to, and hammered against, the swage's upright side; then the *other side* of the tool against the *opposite* upright. The hammer peen must be ground dull to peen out the cone shape in this way, to prevent sharp textures on the steel.

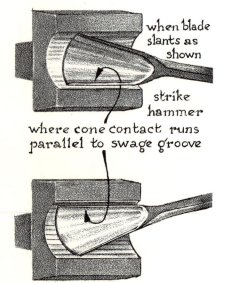

when blade slants as shown
strike hammer
where cone contact runs parallel to swage groove

However, no matter how logical the illustrations and text may seem, in practice this will prove to be a persistently confusing procedure. *It is advisable, therefore, to first make a pattern* that resembles the gouge blade. Cut it out of sheet metal with tinsnips.

Practice hammering this flat mock-up, cold, into a conically shaped blade using a cylindrical swage. Once the technique is mastered, you will understand the correct procedure to follow in order to avoid making typical errors and having to correct them.

CORRECTING COMMON ERRORS IN THE FORGING OF GOUGES

Unfortunately it happens again and again to the beginner that halfway through the project, a good start is ruined by a mistake. A little more thoughtful planning before each move can save the day.

The illustrations show what happens if you fail to aim your hammer blows with precision at the very outset, or if you hold the tool blade slightly slanted in the swage so that a precise central blow then bends it askew.

Another serious error is to use too large a curved hammer with a swage, resulting in the blade being marred by the sharp edges of the swage.

An incorrect alignment between blade and tool shank (an often repeated error) can be corrected by one of the following methods:

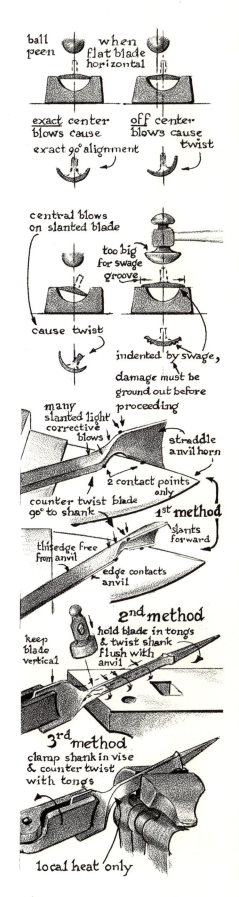

First Method

The more experienced smith can hold the tool diagonally over the horn of the anvil in such a way that a few light but telling hammer blows will twist the blade back into alignment.

Second Method

If the tool is very much out of line, use heavy tongs to hold the cooler part of the blade so their mass acts like a heavy vise. Locally heat the area between the blade and the shank a dark yellow. Hold the blade vertically and hammer the incorrectly slanted shank flush with the anvil facing while holding the blade and tong steady. This then untwists the twist.

Third Method

A similar counter-twisting can be done without the hammer. Clamp the cool shank between the vise jaws, while holding the cool blade firmly with the tongs. The yellow-hot part in between permits you to twist and bring the blade to exactly 90 degrees with the shank upright. In that corrected alignment, quickly "set," and re-shape somewhat (using a light ball-peen hammer) the still hot part, which will have become a little deformed in this twisting action.

Whenever corrections or refinements in forging are called for, you will realize how important it is to apply *very exact* hammer blows, delivered on well-planned locations. It is here that you should make use of every second of the period between heats to judge and plan your next moves. This, combined with skill, makes the good smith. Bad judgment will set you back, no matter how strenuous your hammering may be.

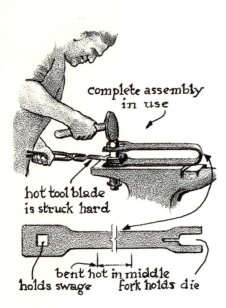

VEINING GOUGE

The forging of a veining gouge can be done *freehand,* but is not as easy as it might seem. Therefore, I have devised a fairly simple way of making this tool with the aid of *dies* held in a spring clamp.

Making a Die Assembly for the Veining Gouge

Use a salvaged car leafspring measuring about 3 inches by ¼ inch in cross section and 40 inches long.

Forge a hole at one end with a square hot punch to match the shank of a V-grooved bottom swage. This end of the steel must be well annealed.

With the abrasive cutoff wheel, cut the other end of the spring clamp lengthwise in half for a distance of 5 inches. Heat it and spread it to form a fork, as shown. This fork must be precisely made, so that its arms are filed *exactly parallel and evenly thick.* Leave it annealed so that the slotted male die can be forced into the fork and held firmly by spring tension.

Install both dies in the prepared ends of the leafspring. Next, heat 6 inches of the exact middle of the spring and, since the die ends remain cool enough to hold by hand, simply bend the spring over, placing one die into the other.

In this position, clamp the die ends firmly between the vise jaws, and rapidly hammer the heated bend into the curve, as shown. The hammering "sets" the spring-clamp position, removing all tensions.

Immediately — before the visible heat glow of the bend has disappeared — transfer the assembly to the anvil, and quickly fasten it with its capscrew and its slanted pipe-spacer. (If it has cooled too much, reheat the bend for this step.)

Now pull the upper arm of the clamp up, just enough so that the hot steel at the bend "gives" a little. When released, the male die should then be spaced about ¼ inch from the female die. If you have pulled it up too much, bear down on it to reseat the male die properly. With a 1-pound hammer, tap with many very light blows all around the bend to remove all tensions.

Release, and check if the ¼-inch spacing between the two die parts has been correctly established. Let all cool slowly.

The ¼-inch spacing allows you to insert the hot tool blank easily and quickly. Also, because of the inherent springiness of the annealed bend, you can pull it up high enough to extract the female die (the swage) in order to replace it with another if needed.

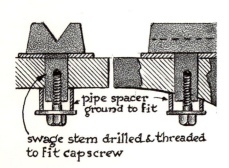

It is important to secure the die assembly *firmly* onto the anvil; any looseness might interfere with the actual forging. To anchor the assembly, drill a hole into the swage shank, as shown, and thread it to fit a ⅜-inch capscrew. The capscrew holds the swage on the anvil with a washer and slanted pipe section. This V-grooved swage acts as the *female* part of the die set. The *male* die is made to match it as follows:

Use a section of a car axle (round or square) measuring about 1¼ inches in cross section. Its working end can be ground to fit the groove of the swage exactly. Slot the die as shown to fit snugly into the forked end of the spring clamp. This arrangement makes it easy to change dies, should it be necessary in making other shapes of gouge blades.

Forging the Gouge Blade

1. Firmly clamp the die assembly to the anvil.
2. Fold the hot blade of the tool blank, as shown, to make sure that the fold and the shank are aligned. This preliminary fold will automatically seek an aligned seating in the bottom die, thus preventing a lopsided positioning between it and the top one.
3. Reheat and insert the hot folded blade while sighting the blank for alignment with the die assembly.
4. With a 3- to 4-pound hammer, deliver a few exactly vertical, heavy blows, *or* many lighter rapid blows, depending on how thick the steel of the blank is.

If all has been constructed correctly, and the forming action done well, the V-gouge blank is ready to be filed, ground, and prepared for tempering.

Note: As an advanced student, you will have noticed by now that if the die surfaces are rough, pitted, or inaccurately matched, every such mark is transferred onto the blank. It means that much work in filing and grinding will have to be done to make up for a poor set of dies. Therefore, if you do decide to spend time making a die assembly, it will pay to make a good one. The die surfaces must be accurate and smooth, exactly aligned, and well tempered.

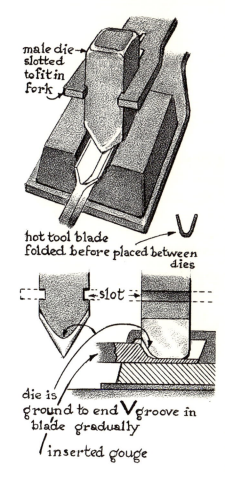

23. Forging a Pair of Pliers

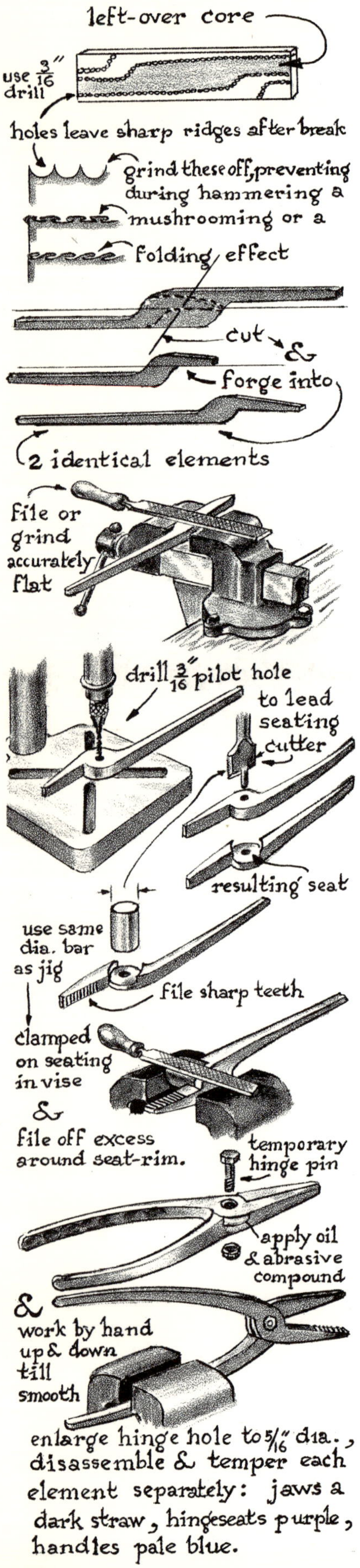

left-over core
use 3/16" drill
holes leave sharp ridges after break
grind these off, preventing during hammering a mushrooming or a folding effect
cut & forge into
2 identical elements
file or grind accurately flat
drill 3/16" pilot hole to lead seating cutter
resulting seat
use same dia. bar as jig
file sharp teeth
clamped on seating in vise & file off excess around seat-rim.
temporary hinge pin
apply oil & abrasive compound
& work by hand up & down till smooth
enlarge hinge hole to 5/16" dia., disassemble & temper each element separately: jaws a dark straw, hingeseats purple, handles pale blue.

For this pair of ½-inch-thick pliers you can use a 4-inch-wide, heavy-caliber leaf of a truck spring.

Cut off a 12-inch section, heat it and flatten it, and then anneal it slowly, buried in ashes.

Scribe off on the steel the curved pattern of the pliers. Along these lines, make evenly spaced center-punch marks for holes to be drilled with a 3/16-inch high-speed drill at slowest speed. The holes must be close enough to leave only *paper-thin* divisions between them. Clamp the core section in the vise and knock off the outer pieces. Use the core section of these pliers. Tie the two outer pieces together with baling wire, and hang them on a nail for future use.

The sharp ridges resulting from the drilling must now be filed off. If they are not removed, they will fold down into the surface during forging. Such flattened ridges would later be revealed again during filing and grinding.

Draw out the stock to form the two plier handles. Then cut the piece in half as shown, and forge the two identical blanks.

Next forge the hinge sections locally into their approximate final dimensions, leaving room for the full diameter of a hinge-seating cutter to mill the bearing sockets.

When the blank for each plier half is finished, refine the flat surfaces on the motor-driven side-grinder. (However, if your skill in flat-filing is sufficient, the pliers' surfaces can be filed perfectly flat by hand.)

Clamp one blank on the drill table. Place a 3/16-inch high-speed drill in the exact punch-marked center of the hinge area, and drill the hole to guide the leading pilot of the seating cutter. Do the same with the other blank.

Each plier half is now ready to be milled with the seating cutter to the depth of exactly one-half the thickness of the plier blank.

In order to fit the two halves together, the excess steel at the *rim* of the hinge-bearing diameter must first be filed off smooth with the aid of a file-jig. The jig is a section of a round bar having the same dimension as the seating cutter. This bar (cut at an exact right angle to its length) is clamped in the vise onto the plier half. File back and forth flush with the bar-jig, removing precisely all excess steel from the rim around the hinge-bearing surface.

Trim the other plier half accurately in the same way. The two halves should now fit together in a temporary assembly. At first they will bind somewhat. To remedy this, smear a coarse-grit valve-grinding compound and some 3-in-One oil over the bearing surfaces. Assemble the plier halves with a temporary hinge pin (use a 3/16-inch-diameter capscrew and nut) holding the two halves lightly together.

Clamp the plier in the vise by one of its handles and work the other half up and down in a "lapping" action, progressively tightening the capscrew a little. The abrasive wears down all minute inaccuracies. Use some kerosene to flush out the metal pulp and abrasive residue. Replenish with fresh abrasive and oil from time to time.

Finish with a finer-grit abrasive and 3-in-One oil. When a smooth, snug fit has been established without binding, take the plier halves apart and clean thoroughly.

Next clamp together with two visegrips the assembled plier, but without the capscrew. Place it on an accurate hardwood prop on the drill-press table. In this position you can enlarge the temporary hole through the hinge area with a $5/16$-inch drill to take a permanent $5/16$-inch-diameter hinge pin.

Each hole, on the outer side of the blanks, is now *countersunk* to a depth of ⅛ inch, as accurately and smoothly as possible. One of the countersunk depressions acts as a bearing surface for the hinge pin, while the other, as a rule, does not move.

Separate the plier halves and temper each one as follows:

1. Heat the jaw and hinge section to a medium cherry red in a slow, clean forge fire and quench in *oil*.

2. Clean off all carbon scale left by the quench using fine-grit carborundum paper. Polish the whole tool, then draw color to dark straw and quench again, this time in *water*.

3. To adjust the temper of the hinge area, use a propane torch or a Bunsen burner gas flame to locally draw the *hinge area only*, very slowly, to peacock color, leaving the jaws a dark straw. Withdraw from flame and let cool slowly.

Assemble the pliers with a temporary hinge pin just long enough to hold the two plier halves snugly together. All remaining inaccuracies can now be ground off on the side grinder, as shown. When all other grinding, refining, and polishing is done, knock out the temporary pin.

Now permanently assemble the pliers, using an accurately fitting $5/16$-inch hinge pin long enough to cold-rivet both heads. (Now you will realize that the better the countersink has been made, the better it will function as a bearing surface.)

Place the assembly flush on the anvil face. The cold-riveting of the hinge pin is done with a ½- to 1-pound ball-peen hammer, using the ball and flat alternately. First the *ball* strikes the whole surface of the pin evenly. Then the *flat* forces down the ridge texture left by the ball. Repeat alternate hammering with ball and flat until complete countersink depression has been filled. Treat the other side the same way.

Any slightly raised surplus material can now be gently ground off without marring the finished surface of the surrounding steel. If you like the appearance of raised, hand-riveted heads, don't grind them off flat, unless they are in the way during use.

If you want to refine the pliers still further, they can be repolished on the buffer to mirror smoothness to prepare them for an application of oxidation color patina to suit your taste (see Chapter 9 on applying color patina). Keep in mind that the jaw and hinge area must not be drawn darker than straw color to ensure that this previously tempered area will remain unchanged in hardness. The handles may vary in color all the way from dark yellow to peacock to blue.

Note that two kinds of pliers are illustrated here. The perfectly symmetrical pair may *look* good but it does not necessarily *work* better than the asymmetrical pair. You will recognize, though, that symmetrical pliers are simpler to make, having identical halves; while the pliers with offset jaws calls for two *different* blanks.

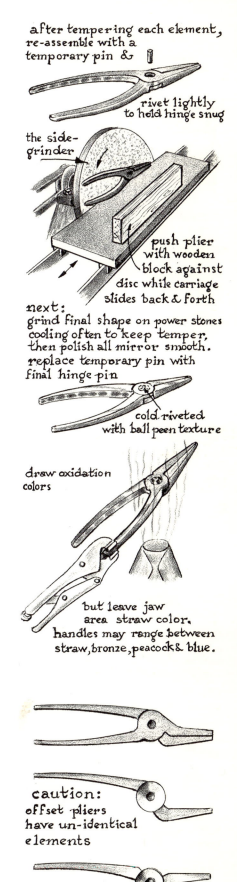

after tempering each element, re-assemble with a temporary pin &

rivet lightly to hold hinge snug

the side-grinder

push plier with wooden block against disc while carriage slides back & forth

next: grind final shape on power stones cooling often to keep temper, then polish all mirror smooth. replace temporary pin with final hinge pin

cold riveted with ball peen texture

draw oxidation colors

but leave jaw area straw color. handles may range between straw, bronze, peacock & blue.

caution: offset pliers have un-identical elements

24. Making a Fireplace Shovel

various sizes & shapes of hammers &

various shape of forming-anvils from salvaged scrap.

flatten after each heating

sand or earth

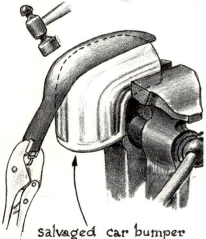

salvaged car bumper part clamped in vise acts as a forming anvil

BASIC PRINCIPLES OF FORMING HEAVY-GAUGE SHEET METAL

Hammering spherical shapes out of mild sheet steel is easiest to do when the metal is yellow hot.

When it is heated locally and hammered over forming pieces improvised from openings in heavy machine parts, such as steel rings, pulleys, cast-iron pipe sections, or any other piece of massive scrap steel, the heated metal can be *stretched* without difficulty.

As the steel yields more and more during stretching, you must reheat and peen out progressively each next area so that hammering will reach every part of it uniformly.

The final shape of the project is reached by hammering it over a mound of sand or earth and scrap parts such as an automobile bumper. (There seems to be an endless variety of shapes in bumper parts, since manufacturers annually change the "sculptural" designs of car models.)

Trim off all superfluous surrounding sheet with a slender cold chisel on the endgrain of a wood stump — a good setup for cutting steel that is too thick for metal shears.

Note: Modern mild steel, used for cold "die-stamping" of auto-body parts, can stand a great deal of cold hammering before breaking. Therefore, much of the mild steel from your scrap pile can be shaped cold. Nevertheless, from time to time you should heat and anneal the cold-hammered parts to avoid breaking the steel.

FORMING A SHOVEL BLADE

The forming of heated sheet metal into a shovel blade, as in the illustrated steps 1 through 5, is a combination of *stretching* and *folding* the steel. Sand or earth, as well as various shapes of heavy scrap steel parts, are used in shaping the blade, as described above. The anvil horn and a choice of bicks placed in the hardy hole are used to hammer out the curves of the handle socket of the shovel.

Both blade and handle socket are formed together, as shown, in a step-by-step process of heating and hammering, reheating and hammering. Final touches can often be applied by cold-hammering and occasional annealing with intermediate reheating.

The handle of this shovel is made of wood from a natural curved section of a tree branch which you may find in piles of orchard prunings, or select and cut in your own garden. First make it fit the handle socket approximately; cut and shape with saw, wood chisel, rasps, plane, and sanding discs.

Then fit it more exactly by burning the hot socket over the handle end. Heat the socket just hot enough to scorch the wood, but not so hot that the smoke will turn into flame. This would char the wood severely. Once it is fitted in, gently tap the end with a hammer to seat the wood evenly. Clamp it between the vise jaws to further pinch it together. While it is in the vise, drill a hole through both socket and wood and countersink it to receive a steel pin. The pin should be long enough to rivet shallow heads flush with the steel of the socket on each end.

Make a ferrule and ring, as shown, to hang the shovel on a wall hook.

Apply a surface finish on the metal by steel-brushing and then waxing or oiling it. Sand the wood handle down as fine as you can, then wax and polish it.

A DECORATIVE STEEL SHOVEL HANDLE

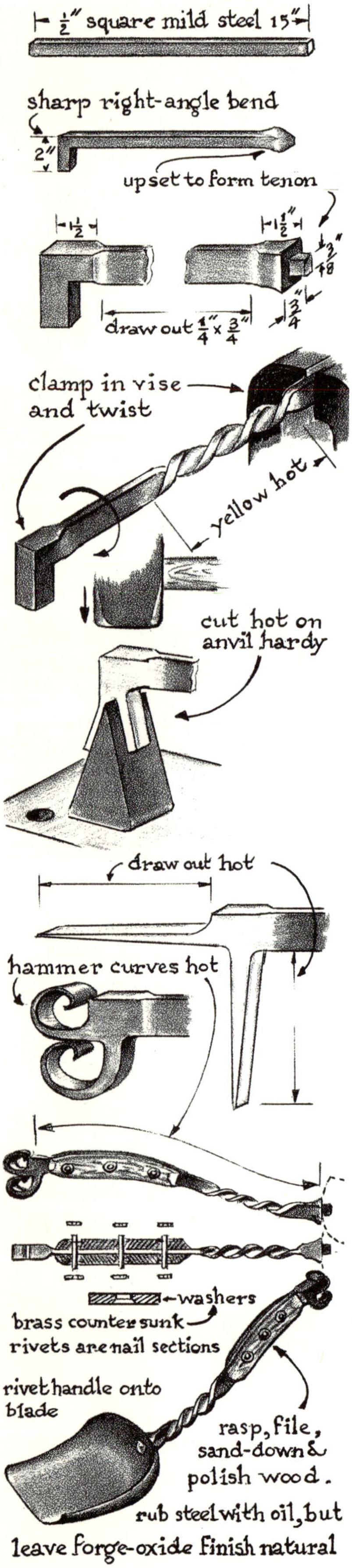

First make a shovel blade in the manner described on page 83.

To make the steel handle as suggested in the accompanying illustration, first upset the steel bar at one end to provide the extra thickness needed for a short shoulder and tenon. The square tenon is forged and filed into shape to fit snugly into a *square hole*. This hole is drilled and filed, or punched, in the shovel blade. In the final assembly, the handle is riveted cold onto the blade.

The decorative design of the handle begins with a right-angle bend. The portion that is to receive the wooden handle-grip is flattened and widened somewhat, as in the illustration. Between the handle and shovel blade, the steel is forged into a rectangular bar ½ inch by ¼ inch in cross section. If the metal is high-carbon steel, this section is most easily twisted *hot*. If it is of mild steel, it may be twisted cold.

Note that the advantage in twisting steel cold is that the perfectly even temperature makes the screw lead evenly spaced. If the metal is heated, the slightest unevenness of heat will make the screw lead unavoidably uneven. However, sometimes such unevenness is desirable, as it gives a hand-rendered character.

The right-angle bend is cut on the anvil hardy as shown. Its two arms are drawn out into slender tapers and curved freehand.

Drill the handle-grip section for the rivets that must hold the two wooden handle sections. Scribe off the hole locations on two identical pieces of hardwood of your choice. With a wood rasp, make these pieces fit approximately on the steel handle. Further perfect the fit by heating the steel, then quickly assembling wood and steel with short pins and clamping these three elements between the vise jaws. The hot steel should scorch the wood, not burn it. Left in the vise jaws to cool, these wood sections will fit to perfection without harming the wood.

To permanently assemble the parts, follow the illustrations. The color of the wood will be brought out when rubbed with beeswax and polished. The steel surfaces can be finished to suit your taste. They can be lightly steel-brushed and oiled to preserve the natural forge black. Or they can be slightly buffed and color-patinated, then sprayed with acrylic as an added rust-resistant.

A LARGE FIREPLACE SHOVEL

Since these shovels never undergo the strains of a garden shovel, the steel stock can be of a modern, malleable type that can be cold-formed easily, once the major deep shapes are hammered out hot.

Anyone well acquainted with the folding characteristics of cloth and of paper is well prepared to plan how to fold and bend sheet metal. Softened by heat, sheet metal yields to shaping in much the same way. The one advantage sheet metal has over paper and cloth is that it can be *stretched* and will maintain the form given it. Therefore, the smith may combine the two possibilities, folding and stretching, in his forming techniques and can make beautifully shaped articles of fairly thick sheet metal. If you have made special hammers of various shapes to curve the blades of woodcarving gouges, these will now come in handy.

First cut out a pattern that is larger than the final blade is to be.

Form the handle socket over a sand or earth mound at first, and further finish it over a bick.

Next, turn the piece over, heat one side of the blade and hammer it upward. Do the same with the other upright of the blade. Form these two uprights to meet the socket portion. Several more local heatings will be needed to blend all curves harmoniously, as in the illustration of the final result.

The separate bottom section of the shovel is also hammered over sand, forming the matching part of the handle socket as well. It must fit the contours of the top half of the blade. Use as many heats as required to make the final shape, as shown.

The wooden handle is made from a curved branch of fine-grained fruit wood. Shape one end of it to fit the finished shovel socket.

If you find that the two shovel sections, placed over the wooden handle end, do not meet precisely, you will now find the malleability of the cold steel to your advantage. Clamp the top and bottom handle sections in the vise with the wooden handle inserted in place.

With the slender cross peen of a lightweight hammer, tap along the creases of the folds of both upper and lower parts. Follow up with shallow rounded ball hammers and smaller flat-faced (slightly crowned) ones. Use these to bend the top and bottom sections together in a tight fit around the wood.

Drill the holes for riveting the two shovel parts together. With a rotary file, trim off the burrs left by the drill, and countersink the holes as deep as the thickness will allow without enlarging the holes. The rivets will then hold firmly, without protruding too much on the outside or inside of the blade.

Short sections of annealed nails that fit the diameter of the holes can serve as rivets. Cold-rivet the shovel parts together while they rest on the anvil face. No grinding or filing will be needed if the length of the rivets is just enough to fill the countersunk holes.

Wherever the bottom piece does not touch the top closely, it can be hammered *between* the spaced rivets, bringing these sections flush together. This forced bending can be neatly done over a large-diameter rounded end of a branch of wood clamped in the vise.

The end of the handle can now be inserted for the permanent fit. Heat the steel blade socket just hot enough to scorch the wood lightly, and hammer the handle into the socket with rapid light blows, using a 1- to 1½-pound hammer. The heated steel will scorch down every interfering unevenness of the wood.

Next, holding the whole assembly together by its handle socket, clamp the uprights of the lower blade section onto the handle between the vise jaws and drill the rivet hole through metal and wood for the holding rivet, which is now installed and headed.

Provide the handle end with a tight-fitting ferrule and crimped-on ring to hang the shovel on a wall hook. Cut the ring from a coil spring and shape hot. Bend the ends out somewhat to reach the ferrule holes. Heat the middle section of the ring, open it, and, after inserting the ends in the ferrule holes, close it between tong jaws.

All surfaces can now be smoothed and finished as in previous similar projects.

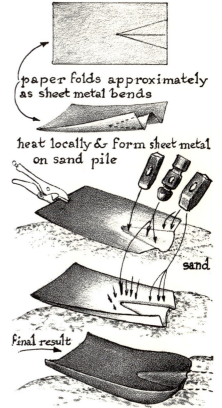

paper folds approximately as sheet metal bends

heat locally & form sheet metal on sand pile

sand

Final result

use any suitable size & shape hammer to draw-out various forms

bottom half of handle-socket riveted onto shovel blade

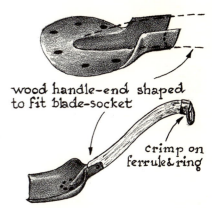

wood handle-end shaped to fit blade-socket

crimp on ferrule & ring

use natural curved fruit tree branches for the shovel handle

25. Making a Small Anvil from a Railroad Rail

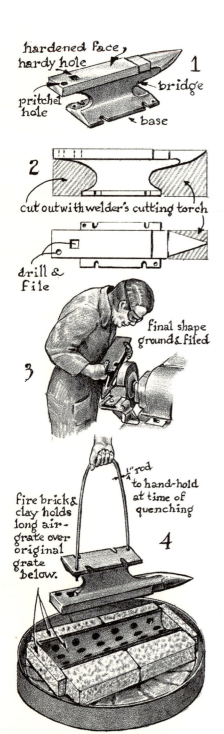

It is of first importance to determine if the salvaged section of a heavy-gauge railroad rail is of temperable quality. Illustration 2 shows where the welder must cut out the sections not needed. (Save these for your scrap pile, however, so they can be used for future projects.) To test the temperability of the steel, heat one of the waste sections to a cherry red and quench in water. File-test it, and if it has become brittle-hard, you will know that you can make of the blank a fine, well-tempered anvil large enough to hammer out most forgings made in the average hobby shop.

The design of the anvil in the illustration should be followed closely. The large, 1 hp motor-grinder with 12-inch-diameter hard, coarse-grit wheel will enable you to grind the proper shape of the horn and flat surfaces (3), instead of hand-filing them. The anvil face should be smooth and polished.

Since the steel comes more or less annealed, you can drill the pritchel hole. Next, the larger hole for the hardies must first be drilled and then filed into a square. The four holes, or notches, in the base are to bolt the anvil down on a wood stump. Two small holes in the base are drilled for a temporary handle with which it can be lifted when being tempered.

Since this anvil is too long to heat *evenly* for tempering in a small, centrally heated forge fire, it will be necessary to convert the forge temporarily (see illustration 4.)

To make a *long* air grate, I have found it practical to use a salvaged broken 4-inch-diameter cast-iron plumbing pipe. Cut a 14- to 16-inch section lengthwise on the abrasive cutoff wheel or mechanical saw (if you have one). Drill a dozen or more ⅜-inch holes, evenly distributed, to form an elongated air grate.

Surround this grate with firebrick, as shown. Dry, porous building bricks could also be used for a temporary project such as this. But make sure they are *dry,* as they might explode during heating if moist and not porous enough.

Plug all remaining air passages around the bricks with fire clay so that the air can reach only the long mound of coals over the grate.

Prepare to handle the anvil *upside down* by fastening a ¼-inch-diameter bent rod to the base as a yoke. Thread the rod ends for ¼-inch nuts and slip them through the holes in the base of the anvil. Make the handle long enough so that your hand is far from the fire (about 2 feet above the anvil).

Before you start the fire for tempering the anvil, be sure to have a 50-gallon drum full of water ready to quench it. Also have ready a shallow tray with an inch of water to cool the anvil face.

Make a *clean* fire with at least a 4-inch-thick layer of hot coals. Carefully place the anvil upside down on it and, with the poker, bank the coals over its "head." Cover the fire with sections of dry asbestos cement sheet (see illustrations 5 and 6). This is a practical and efficient way to enclose the fire and these sheets are often available as waste material at building-supply yards. Sheet metal, of course, would do, but its heat radiation would be uncomfortable.

It may take an hour with an even, slow, and low heat to bring this bulky piece of steel to medium cherry red heat. From time to time lift and peer underneath the asbestos cement sheets to check how the heating of the steel has progressed. Rake a little added coal to keep up the fire, when necessary, and continue the heating by cranking the air steadily, but *very slowly*. If the blower is driven by an electric fan, control the air flow to maintain this very slow, steady heat.

As soon as the moment arrives to quench, cool the top of the yoke handle with a wet rag to be able to hand-hold it. Remove the asbestos sheets and rake the coals away. Lift the hot anvil from the fire. (The exposed fire now is radiating much heat and should be quickly covered again with the asbestos sheets to make certain that nothing around it will catch fire.

Plunge the anvil into the 50-gallon drum filled with water. Sink it as deep as you can reach, while pumping the anvil up and down. This cools the steel fastest and makes the hardness penetrate the anvil face as deep as it can get (7).

Clean the anvil face of its scales and carbon, and restore the polish until it shines like a mirror. Replace the yoke handle by another one, attached as shown in illustration 8. The anvil now stands right side up.

Clean the slag out of the fire and replenish it with fresh coal evenly spread over its full length. You need a lesser fire this time; it must give just enough heat for the temper colors of light bronze or dark straw to appear on the face of the anvil.

Wait for the fire to become clean and smokeless once more. Place the anvil, suspended right side up, on the bed of hot coals. Cover it with the asbestos shields, leaving a ¼-inch space between the sheets and bridge of the anvil (see illustration 8). This allows the fire's heat to flow *evenly under and around the anvil head,* which has remained free from direct contact with the fire. The anvil horn may be ignored for the time being because it will be annealed separately later on.

Since the heat flow should be even and very slow, fan the fire only very gently. Watch for the slightest faint straw color to appear on the anvil face. It is now important to shift the hot coals with the poker to any spot below the anvil where the polished anvil face has not yet begun to show the faint straw color. This is to try to even up the distribution of the heat flow. As long as the heating of the anvil body is very, very slow, such corrective measures will be effective.

hot coals 3" layer below anvil & around

horn to stay relatively cool

5

plug with clay all open spaces

blocked-in fire shown with sheet asbestos or asb. cement shingles

6

leave ¼" space around anvil bridge

a very slow, even heat is kept. at moment that anvil body has become cherry red,

lift out & quench

50 gallons water

7

next polish anvil face mirror smooth &

place in fire that is at low heat & blocked-in as shown

8

the steady low heat gradually reaches anvil facing, showing temper colors. When straw yellow, place upside down in in shallow water & let cool

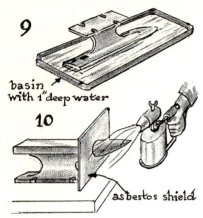

after torch flame anneals horn to pale blue, let all cool slowly.

When, at last, the color is drawn evenly over the whole anvil face to a dark straw or light bronze, lift the anvil by its strap handle, and with tongs, carefully tumble it upside down. Quickly, in this position, lift it, with a tong in each hand, and place it in a shallow tray of water (9). The anvil face is thus prevented from being further heated through conductivity by the remaining stored heat in the anvil base and bridge.

Now leave the whole to cool slowly. Once cooled, the horn, which always is to remain soft, can be annealed separately, as shown in illustration 10.

I have made four small anvils in this way. Each one was of high quality with a hard, tough anvil face and softer annealed horn. They have proved to be as good as any larger commercial anvils I have ever had. I bolt them firmly on a heavy wood stump and ignore their light caliber, using them as if they were 100-pounders.

26. The Power Hammer

down pressure controls degree of speed of hammer movement as well as force of blows, based on belt slippage to full run

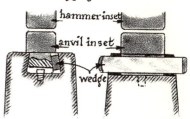

anvil & hammer-sets have identical footing

flattening peening forming

infinite variety insets possible to suit one's need

curving cutting tapering

gouge blanks easily forged on a power hammer with special insets

The value gained in using a power hammer is mainly in drawing out heavy-gauge steel from thick into thin, short into long, and narrow into wide, without much physical effort.

Sometimes the power hammer can also help in upsetting thin steel into thick, but this is quite tricky to do because a heavy blow will buckle thin upright parts, and a lighter blow will not penetrate to the center. As a result, a cauliflowering of the edges of the thin upright takes place, and this must be flattened immediately again if folding is to be avoided. If a fold is detected, it must be ground or filed out before proceeding.

Of course, repeated cauliflowering and flattening at long last does make the total dimension a little thicker. But again, the trickiness of this operation will generally cause you to abandon the attempt and to start all over again with heavier stock. In time you will learn that there is a limit to the upsetting of thin stock.

You can extend the uses of a power hammer by making special hammer and anvil inserts. With these you can form, with a few blows, a gouge blade for instance, which otherwise would have taken you half an hour or more to forge by hand.

A whole book could be written for the hobbyist on the use of the small power hammer. But it is my belief that this elaboration is not called for here. The reason is that by the time the student has diligently practiced the making of the projects offered in the foregoing pages, he will be fully prepared to judge whether he will benefit from adding this machine to his equipment.

My personal experience has been that the power hammer has been useful when I needed a sledger-helper. So my admonition remains: Learn first all that a blacksmith must know about freehand forging; only after that will you be able to make the greatest use of the machine as a time-and-muscle-saver *while remaining in full control of it.*

Do not underestimate the danger of machine-hypnosis. It is a trap which you must try to avoid falling into. Often the less-talented, the commercially oriented, the non-artist, and the vocational machine operator yield to this hypnosis.

I recognize, however, that for the making of mass-produced items that lend themselves to power-hammer treatment, you can increase your chances of earning a livelihood with it. Should this come about, all that you have learned to do in blacksmithing *without* the machine will enhance your work. At the same time, you will have the satisfaction of knowing you could do as good a job with the simple use of a fire, a hammer, and an anvil.

Logic, skill, and common sense, which are a good blacksmith's attributes, will guide you from now on when untried steps must be taken. You will discover, with pleasure and satisfaction, that you have become your own teacher.

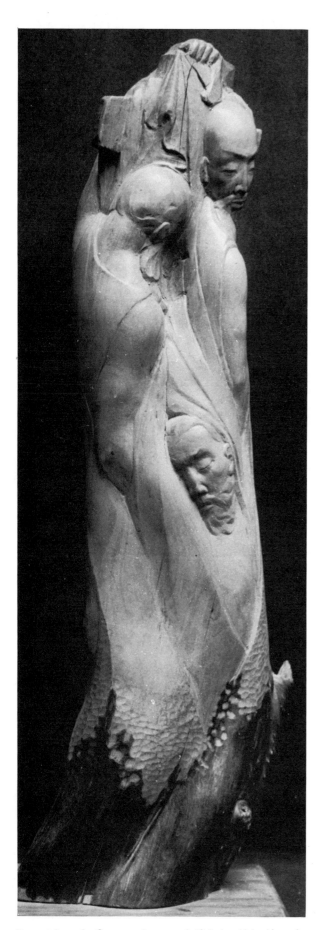

Left: **Maylaya,** lifesize, carved by the author in Java with the tools he forged in the native blacksmith shop described on page 8. *Right:* Endgrain wood engraving, cut with traditional engraver's burins which serve as a basis for the design of small woodcarving gouges, as shown on opposite page.

Bali Mother and Child, carved in sandstone with one-point and claw stonecarving tools described on page 46. Weyger's sculptures are all direct carvings, done without benefit of prestudies, drawings, models, or measuring devices. Photo: Jim Ziegler.

Descent from the Cross, madrone wood, 12 inches high, Alexander G. Weygers. This piece was carved with small hand gouges like those shown on page 91.

Sister Joanne, O.P., art teacher at Dominican College, San Rafael, Calif., a pupil learning to handforge stonecarving tools at Weyger's blacksmith shop. Photo: Jim Ziegler.

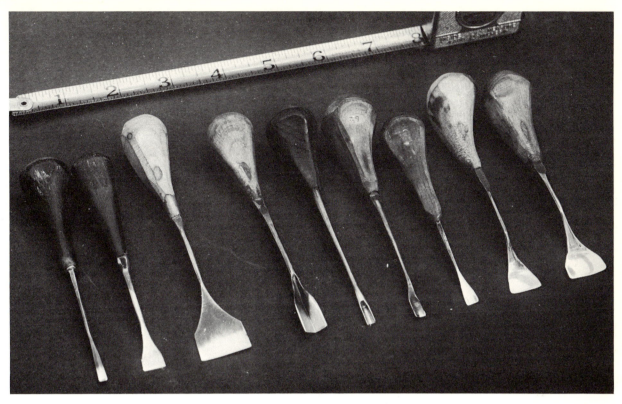

These small woodcarving gouges are designed to be manipulated in the manner of engravers' burins.

Above left: Peter Partch, a student, carves a low relief in marble using his own forged carving chisels. Photo: Jim Ziegler.

Above right: The inner bowl cavity was carved with the special tool shown. Standard sculpture gouges were used for carving the outside.

Right: Collection of tools forged by the author's students during a three-week sculpture workshop. Photo: Jim Ziegler.

Typical blacksmith tools: 1 hammers, various weights and shapes / **2** tongs, various sizes and shapes / **3** hot punches, square- and round-ended / **4** stonecarving hammers, various weights (mild steel) / **6** cone-shaped bottom swage and matching fuller, to form blades of woodcarving gouges / **7, 8** angle-shaped swage and matching fuller, to form blades of large and small V-shaped carving gouges / **9** die to form a reinforcement rib in gouge or garden-tool blade / **11** jigs which may be clamped between vise jaws / **12** set-hammer or flatter / **14** hardy / **15** hot chisel / **17** top swage / **18** heading plate with holes of various sizes to form bolt heads (from 3/4-inch-thick scrap steel) / **19** car-hitch ball, used as forming head to shape curved blades of implements / **20** drift pin to enlarge holes started by hot punches / **21** upsetting matrix made from a section of a heavy truck axle; fits hardy hole of a large anvil / **22** squared section of a heavy truck axle from which a blacksmith hammer is to be made / **23** remnant of a heavy truck axle.

Samples of scrap steel for the modern blacksmith: 1 section of a car bumper / **2, 21** coil spring of a car / **3** section of a plow disc cut with welding torch / **4** half a 4-inch-diameter cast-iron plumbing pipe / **5** angle iron from bed frame / **6** section of a broken pick axe / **7** parts of a steering-gear rod / **8** set of car leaf springs / **9** half of a large ball-bearing race / **10** old wood-splitting wedge / **11** bent 1- x 5/16-inch bar / **12** old flat file / **13** section of a car bumper / **14, 22** old phonograph spring / **15** farm machinery spikes / **16** large bolt nut / **17** hub socket wrench / **18** motor valves / **19** industrial hacksaw blade / **20** cast-iron valve-box lid / **23** ½-inch round bar / **24** large tie-bolt washer / **25, 39** die parts / **26** half of compound shear / **27** old carpenter's flat chisel / **28** hub socket wrench / **29** double magnet / **30** lever linkage / **31** cast-iron bridge shoe / **32** ball-bearing thrust washer / **33** broken crowbar / **34** farm machine cutter blades / **35** engine pushrods / **37** old Ford car magnet / **38** thrust block / **40, 44** old wrench / **42** collar / **43** screwdriver blank / **45** hay-rake tine / **46** scrap-steel-plate remnant / **47** 1- x 1-inch high-carbon-steel bar from a harvester's drive shaft / **48** part of a carpenter's handsaw / **49** shaft end and bevel gear / **50** part of a car stick shift, and lawnmower blade / **51** ball bearings / **52** antique car springs / **53** car linkage bar.

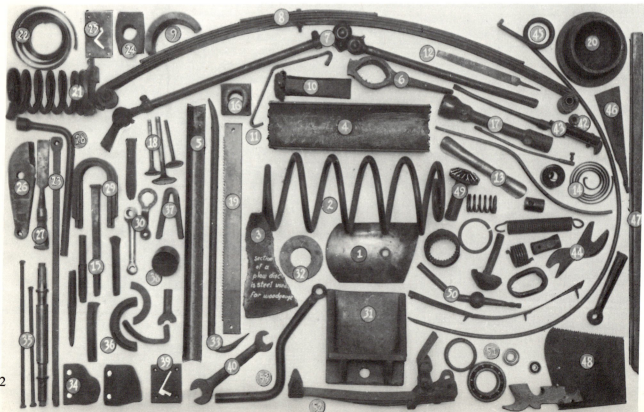

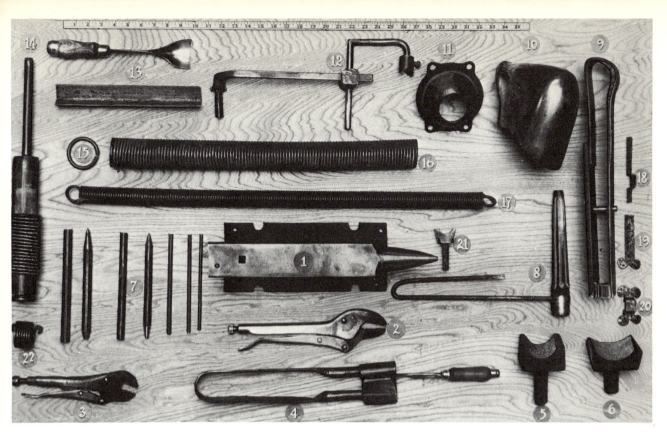

Modern and traditional blacksmith tools and scrap-steel stock: 1 small anvil (hardened face) made from a section of heavy-gauge railroad rail / **2, 3** self-locking pliers (modern vise-grip) / **4** hand-held die-set to form small, round woodcarving gouge blade / **5** standard large cylindrically ground bottom swage, used as stock to make # 6 / **6** special wide-curved cone-shaped blade for a large woodcarving gouge / **7** various sizes of high-carbon-steel rods to make one-point stonecarving tools / **8** hexagon die punch to shape hexagon holes in making box wrenches / **9** hand-held die-set to form keepers for door latches / **10** part of car bumper, which, when clamped in vise, acts as a forming block over which curves are shaped for blades of gouges, shovels, etc. / **11** salvaged spherical section of a ball-joint housing to act as forming block to shape curves / **12** universal hold-down tool / **13** section of a high-carbon bed frame that was used as stock for wood gouge (# 6) / **14** jig, clamped in vise, serves to uncoil heated coil springs into straight rods / **15** single winding of a coil spring / **16, 17** salvaged coil springs from which to make high-carbon, straight steel rod, used as stock for forging small artifacts / **18, 19, 20** keeper blank, forged into final shape / **21** bottom swage made to fit anvil (# 1).

Useful items forged from scrap steel and special hammers used to form shovel blades and gouges: 1 one-piece fireplace tong / **2, 10** fireplace pokers / **3, 8, 9** fireplace shovels / **6** stove-lid lifter / **11, 12, 4** hammers converted from standard hammer heads, to shape special curves into specially made forming swages.

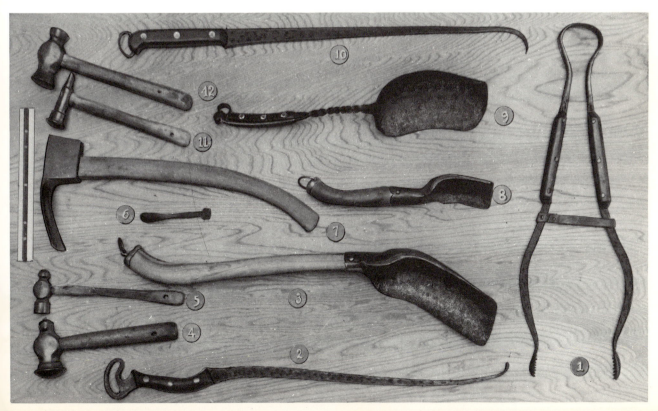

Glossary

ADAPTER. A driven instrument made to fit one type (size) of tool at one end and another type (size) at the other end.
AGITATOR. See *Paint Mixer*.
ALIGNMENT. In line with another element; not askew in relation to it.
ALLOY. A compound or fusion of two or more metals.
ANGLE IRON. Steel bars which have a cross-section of an angle (usually 90°). The iron, in this term, is a holdover from the days before iron was made into steel. Now all angle iron is actually steel, either mild or high-carbon steel.
ANNEAL. To soften steel through slow cooling after enough heat has made the steel lose its brittleness.
ARBOR. A wheel, axle, or shaft rotating in one or more bearings held by a frame that is bolted down.
AUGER. A wood drill, as a rule over 1½ inches in diameter. (Also may refer to augers to drill holes in earth.)
BASTARD FILE. A file with teeth coarser than a smooth file and less coarse than a coarse file.
BEVEL. In cutting tools, the facet that has been ground at the cutting edge (inside and outside *bevels*).
BLANK. The rough shape of a tool before filing, grinding, etc. has prepared the tool for tempering and assembly with the handle.
BOSS. A locally raised part of steel.
BRITTLE QUENCH. See *Quench*.
BUFFER. A cotton wheel used to polish surfaces.
BUFFING WHEEL. A motor-driven cotton wheel that rotates at high speed. A buffing compound rubbed into the cotton buffs (polishes) the steel held against the wheel.
BUNSEN BURNER. A gas burner with a single blue flame used in laboratories to heat liquids and objects.
BURIN. The cutting tool of an engraver.
BURR. A small rotary file, often used to take off a *burr* left on the edge of steel by previous cutting. A *burr* may also be the "feather-edge" left on a tool's cutting edge in the final step of sharpening the tool.
BUSH HAMMER. A tool with a hammer face having 9 or more raised points which, on impact, crush or pulverize the surface of stone. From the French *boucher:* to crush, to eat, to bite. The bush *tool* also has 9 or more raised points which, when hammered upon, crush or pulverize the surface of stone.
BUTTERFLY-CENTER. A lathe-center insert placed in headstock that has four sharp wings and a center pin which press into the wood that is to be turned on a wood lathe.
CAP SCREW (OR TAP-BOLT). A bolt (without its nut) screwed into a threaded hole of one part, to hold another part clamped onto the first.
CAPE CHISEL. A narrow chisel that cuts deep grooves, specifically key slots, in steel.
CARBIDE-TIP. An extremely hard tip soldered on to the end of a regular high-carbon steel bar used to turn wood or steel on a lathe.
CARRIAGE BOLT. A bolt which ties together wooden members in structures. It has a square section under the head to keep the bolt from turning.

CASE HARDENING. The process of applying a skin-deep hardness to the outer surface of mild steel in a forge fire.
CENTER-PUNCH. Tool used to make a "center" mark for locations to be drilled, or to mark off pattern outlines on steel.
CHASING TOOLS. Tools used to make marks (raised or depressed) in metal surfaces to create texture.
CHECKING (of wood). The splitting of wood during drying.
CHISEL. A metal tool with a blade having a sharp-edged end; used for cutting wood, stone, metal, or other material.
CHISEL, CARPENTER'S WOOD. A flat chisel for cutting wood.
CHISEL, COLD. A chisel that may be used on *cold* annealed steel to cut it.
CHISEL, HOT. A chisel used to cut *yellow hot* steel. The steel is cut with the hot chisel on the soft anvil table or a mild-steel plate placed over the hard anvil face. The chisel is either a hand-held long cold chisel or a sturdy chisel head fastened to a long wooden stem.
CHUCK. A clamp screwed on a rotating shaft to fasten drills, small grinders, etc.
CLAW. A multiple-toothed stonecarving tool used to refine the rough texture left by the one-point tool.
COEFFICIENT OF CONDUCTIVITY. A number that indicates the degree of speed at which heat is conducted from one spot to the next in a type of steel.
COIL SPRINGS. Springs made of long, high-carbon steel rods that are wound hot around a bar and afterward tempered the hardness for which such springs are designed.
COKE. The substance fresh coal becomes after heat has driven out all elements that give off smoke and yellow flame. Coke resembles charcoal in that it gives off a blue flame and lights easily.
COLLAR. A steel ring, often mounted on a shaft with a set screw.
CONDUIT PIPE. Galvanized steel pipe through which electricians install electric wires.
COUNTERSINK. A cone-shaped, large *drill bit* used to bevel the edge of a sharp-edged cylindrical hole left by a smaller drill; a shallow cylindrical depression around a hole, larger than the hole in diameter.
CUTOFF WHEEL. A thin abrasive wheel that cuts steel too hard to cut with a hacksaw.
DIE. A two-part mold (male and female) used for making and reproducing a form one or more times. The material is held between the dies that are then forced together to produce the form or shape that the dies have at their contacting planes. Dies are used strictly to mass-produce articles or to make an article that is too complicated to make easily by hand. (Also, a matrix.)
DRIFT. A tapered steel pin which is driven into a hole in stone to split it. Another use is to pull together two slightly unmatched holes in two plates to align them perfectly.
DOWEL (STEEL). A locking-pin that holds parts and keeps them from shifting their positions.
DRAWING TEMPER COLOR. Reheating brittle-quenched steel that has been polished to see the oxidation color spectrum (temper colors) clearly. Once this color spectrum appears and the wanted color, which corresponds to its *hardness*, has been "drawn," the tool is quenched.

DRAWING OUT STEEL. *Stretching* steel, making it longer or wider or both. The opposite is to upset steel, making it thicker and/or shorter.
DRESSER. A tool that cuts or wears down the surface of grindstones.
DRESSING. Making an inaccurate grinding wheel accurate with a dresser by wearing the wheel surface down to exact shape.
DRILL BIT. Could be called a *drill*, but generally this term refers to a local bit at end of a plain drill rod. Such bits may be of varied designs to meet various drilling problems.
DRILL PRESS. A machine for drilling holes in metal or other material.
EMBOSS. To raise steel locally with bosses. The *boss* is a form of die which, pressed or hammered into the steel plate from one side, raises the steel surface on the other side of the sheet.
EYEBOLT. A bolt which has a hole in a round, flattened end instead of the hexagon, or round, or square-bolt head.
FACE. Generally refers to a flat surface on the sides or top of a tool or machine part: an anvil face, side-face, the face of a disc, "to face" a surface, when grinding, milling, and cutting steel surfaces.
FERRULE. A metal ring, cap, or tube-section placed on the end of a handle to keep it from splitting.
FIREBRICK. A brick which withstands high temperatures as in brick-lined kilns and fireplaces.
FIRECLAY. A clay which will not crack when fired.
FLASH FIRE. A fire that starts suddenly when an inflammable liquid reaches a heat corresponding to its "flash" point, setting the liquid aflame.
FLATTER. A tool shaped like a hammer head but with an accurate, square, flat face at one end and a crowned end at the other that can be struck with a heavy hammer. The flatter's face, placed on a heated inaccurate flat section of a workpiece lying on the anvil, can flatten it out accurately.
FORGE. A furnace in which steel is heated.
FREEZING. The bonding together of two clamped-together steel parts that have corroded or have been forcefully locked together. To break this bond is a frequent chore when taking rusted machinery apart.
FULLER. A blacksmith's tool that fits in the hardy hole of the anvil (bottom fuller), or is fastened on a long wooden stem (top fuller) in order to groove steel, draw it out, or "set" rounded corners. Comes in various sizes.
GAUGE. A specific size in reference to steel sheet or bar thickness, nail size, etc.
HACKSAW. A hand saw with narrow blade set in metal frame, used to cut metal.
HARDY. An anvil insert that acts as a cutter of hot steel. Also called hardies are hardy-type tools that fit in the hardy hole, but have other special names, as a rule, i.e., *fullers*.
HARDY HOLE. The square hole in the anvil that the hardy fits into.
HEADING PLATE. A thick, flat piece of steel with a slightly tapered hole in the middle which receives a rod that has been upset at the end. The hot end can then be hammered into a head.
HEADSTOCK. The rotating driver end of a lathe.
HEAT. The period that the hot steel, removed from the fire, maintains its forging heat.

HEATING. The period of heating the steel.
HEAT TREATING. The process of *tempering* steel for a specific hardness; can also refer to treating steel to bring about a specific softness.
HIGH-CARBON STEEL. A temperable steel, primarily used to harden such steels for specific hardness in the process called "tempering." In industry, steel of over 0.2% carbon.
HOLD-DOWN OR HOLD-FAST. A contrivance for holding the heated workpiece to be forged when the smith needs both hands free to manipulate his tools. One end of the hold-down is rammed into the anvil's hardy or pritchel hole so that its other end will hold down (or hold fast) the workpiece.
HOLLOW GRIND. To grind the bevel of a cutting tool concave.
HONING. Grinding a steel surface with a *honing stone*. This stone leaves an almost-polished surface.
HP (HORSEPOWER). A unit of power, used in stating the power required to drive machinery.
JIG. A device which acts as a guide to accurately machine-file, fold, bend, or form a workpiece. This is used if lack of skill handicaps the worker in making the workpiece. Such jigs guide him and also save time in mass production of tools.
KEEPER. The part of a door latch through which the latch bolt slides.
LAPPING. An abrasive action in which a grinding compound is used between two surfaces that, when held pressed together in movement, grind themselves into one another.
LATHE. A machine for shaping articles which causes them to revolve while acted upon by a cutting tool.
LEAF SPRING. A spring with an oblong cross-section and a sufficient length to act as a spring. Automobiles as a rule use such springs singly or in graduated layers to suspend the car body over the axles.
LOW-CARBON STEEL. A steel that is not temperable, which contains less than 0.2% carbon.
MALL. A large hammer with wooden head, sometimes steel-weighted, used to drive stakes in the ground.
MALLEABLE. Capable of being shaped or worked by hammering, etc.
MALLET. A wooden hammer-head on a short handle used to hammer on wood-carving gouges. Sometimes the mallet head is made of rawhide or plastic or hard rubber.
MATRIX. A female die in which a malleable substance may be formed by pressing to fill it. A cavity in which anything is formed or cast.
MILD STEEL. A low-carbon steel. It is not temperable.
MILLING CUTTER. See *Seating Cutter*.
NAIL SET. A tool resembling a center-punch but with a hardened, cup-shaped end instead of a ground point. This cup-shaped end, placed on the nail head center, keeps the tool from slipping sideways while "setting" the nail.
OFFSET. The step down (or up) in a bar or plate from its original alignment into another alignment, as a rule, parallel with it.
ONE-POINT TOOL. The basic stonecarving tool that "chips" stone in the first roughing-out action of stonecarving.

OXIDATION COLOR SPECTRUM. The color spectrum that results from the oxidation of cold steel as it gradually gets hot. The polished metal sheen shows the colors as clearly as the color spectrum in rainbows.
PAINT MIXER (AGITATOR). A rod with a crooked end which, rotated in the paint, mixes it.
PATINA. The colored oxidation on metal surfaces. It results during the process of tempering the metal. (On bronze and many other metals, a patina comes about after long exposure to oxygen of the air and chemicals.)
PEARL GRAY. A typical file color. When high-carbon steel emerges from a quench, pearl gray indicates "file hardness."
PEEN END. A hammer with a wedge-shaped, round-edged end or a half-sphere ball end used to stretch steel by indentation. A *cross peen* hammer has the rounded edge of the peen at 90° to the hammer stem.
PRITCHEL HOLE. The round hole next to the square hardy hole in the anvil.
PUSH-ROD. The rod in an engine which "pushes" a valve to open the cylinder for the intake or expulsion of its gases.
QUENCH. To cool hot steel in a liquid. *Brittle quenching* is the act of cooling high-carbon steel at its critical heat at its fastest so that it will emerge brittle-hard.
QUENCHING BATH. The liquid into which the hot steel is dipped or immersed to cool it.
RASP. A coarse file used mostly to grate or tear softer materials such as wood, horn, plaster of Paris, and soft stones that are not abrasive.
RHEOSTAT. An instrument which may be adjusted to let more, or less, electric current pass, for instance, to regulate the speed of an electric motor or to dim or brighten a light bulb.
ROUT. To cut or scoop out material with a router tool.
SADDLE. A rounded piece of steel on which to form another piece in its shape.
SCRIBE. A sharp-pointed steel marking pin used to scratch a line on to a workpiece.
SEATING CUTTER. Tool used to cut a *seat* in a part onto which another part fits exactly. The cutting also may be called *milling,* and the cutter then would be a *milling cutter.*
SET HAMMER. A hammer head fastened on a long wooden stem resembling a flatter. Placed on a partly formed section of a workpiece, it *sets* it into its final position when a regular hammer delivers a blow on it.
SET SCREW. A screw that clamps or *sets* one part onto another part.
SHANK. The part of a tool between tang and blade.
SHOULDER. In craft usage, an abrupt wider or thicker dimension in rod or shaft against which another part rests.
SLAG. A melted mix of non-combustible matter in coal. It lumps together.
SLEDGE. A heavy (6-pound or more) hammer on a long stem, used by the blacksmith's helper using both his hands, for heavy hammering of heavy steel.
SLEEVE. In bearings, the bushing; a precisely honed bronze tube that fits the shaft it bears.
SPECTRUM. A division of colors occurring on the shiny part of steel when it is heated for tempering; similar to the rainbow colors seen through a prism.
SPRING STEEL. A high-carbon steel tempered so that it will act as a spring.
STEEL PLATE. Refers to flat sheets of steel thicker than $3/16$ of an inch. It is optional at what thickness or thinness metal may be called sheet metal. Example: boilers are made of plate steel; stovepipes are made of sheet metal.

STEEL STOCK. The supply of steel from which an item is selected to forge, or machine, or grind the workpiece to be made.
STROPPING. The final step in sharpening a cutting edge on a leather strop.
SWAGE. The "saddle" that is grooved to form steel and fits into the anvil's hardy hole (bottom swage), and a similar tool, fastened to a long wooden stem, placed *over* steel to form it (top swage).
TAILSTOCK. The center pin in the stationary end of the lathe that holds the rotating metal, wood or other material between the two lathe centers.
TANG. The part of the tool blank that is locked into the tool handle.
TEMPERABLE STEEL. A steel of a higher than 0.2% carbon quality which can be *tempered.*
TEMPERING. In forging metal, the process to arrive at a specific hardness of high-carbon steel.
TEMPLATE. A pattern, often made from cardboard or sheet metal, to serve as a model, the outline of which is scribed on the steel to be cut.
TINSNIPS. Sturdy, short-bladed shears that cut sheet metal.
TOOL REST (OR TOOL POST). As a rule, those parts on machines onto which a tool is held down firmly to be ground down. Also may refer to the clamp on a machine to hold a cutting tool.
TRIPOLI. An abrasive-impregnated wax compound that, when rubbed into a rotating cotton buffing wheel, acts as the finest steel polisher.
UPSETTING. The process of making a piece of steel shorter and thicker.
VEINING TOOL. A V-shaped gouge that cuts V grooves referred to as "veins."
VISE. A two-jawed screw clamp bolted to the workbench to hold things steady while being worked.
VISEGRIP PLIERS. Self-locking pliers.
WELD. To fuse metals together under heat.
WROUGHT IRON. Iron that has been worked in a "puddling" process to purify it. It contains no carbon and is least subject to rusting. It is rarely used today, and hence not found in scrap piles. It can be welded easily and will not burn during melting as does steel.